Canon Peter Harvey mi
for more than 50 yea
national church mag
World, and continued to write even as ill-health took
its toll in later years. He also enjoyed work as a
pilgrimage leader and visited the Holy Land more
than 20 times.

He was married twice, to Vivienne who died in
1978, and to Betty who cared for him until his death.
He had six children from his first marriage.

GLORY, LAUD

—— AND ——

HONOUR

*Favourite hymns
and their stories*

PETER HARVEY

TRIANGLE

First published in Great Britain in 1996
Triangle
SPCK
Holy Trinity Church
Marylebone Road
London NW1 4DU

ACKNOWLEDGEMENTS
Bible quotations are from the Revised Standard Version of the Bible
© 1971 and 1952.

Some of the hymn stories in this book have already appeared in various
publications, including: *The Church of England Newspaper*, *The Methodist
Recorder*, *The Church Observer*, *The Chichester Diocesan Magazine*,
The Anglican Digest (USA), *The Welsh Churchman* and a number of
other parish publications in Kent and Sussex and surrounding areas.

The publishers and author have made every attempt to contact
copyright holders for the use of material in this book. If copyright
material has been used inadvertently without permission,
the publishers would be delighted to hear from those concerned.

British Library Cataloguing-in-Publication Data
A catalogue record for this book is available from the British Library

ISBN 0–281–04963–7

Typeset by Wilmaset Ltd, Birkenhead, Wirral
Printed and bound in Great Britain by
BPC Paperbacks Ltd.

Contents

ACKNOWLEDGEMENTS

With thanks to my dear wife, Betty, without whose help this book could not have been published.

INTRODUCTION

Most of us are familiar with hymn-singing in one way or another. Some like to do it every Sunday, others more occasionally on special occasions, such as weddings or funerals. Everyone has their favourite, often because of a well-loved tune or because it brings back memories. But we often know little about our favourites: who wrote them and who composed the tunes? And many of the stories are well worth the telling! Hymnody in general is a fascinating subject, reflecting not only the fundamentals of our faith but also church history in the lives of the authors and composers, as well as covering 'all the changing scenes of life'. Charlotte Elliott's priest brother said that her great hymn *Just as I am, without one plea* did much more to spread the gospel than all his sermons put together throughout his entire ministry. This is why, with the valued assistance of the church press and dioceses, I carried out a nationwide poll of favourite hymns, contacting people and parishes, with a wide variety of church background and spread over all age groups. The Top Twenty were as follows:

1 *Dear Lord and Father of mankind*
2 *Praise, my soul, the King of heaven*
3 *The day thou gavest, Lord, is ended*
4 *When I survey the wondrous Cross*
5 *Love divine, all loves excelling*
6 *O Jesus, I have promised*
7 *Abide with me*
8 *Guide me, O thou great Redeemer*
9 *At the name of Jesus*
10 *Just as I am, without one plea*
11 *The King of love my Shepherd is*
12 *Glorious things of thee are spoken*
13 *Thine be the glory*

14 *And did those feet in ancient time*
15 *Lord Jesus Christ, you have come to us*
16 *There is a green hill far away*
17 *Onward, Christian soldiers*
18 *Let all mortal flesh keep silence*
19 *Lead us, heavenly Father, lead us*
20 *The Lord's my Shepherd, I'll not want*

Other favourites included:

God be in my head and in my understanding
Come down, O Love divine
My song is love unknown
For the beauty of the earth
Tell out, my soul, the greatness of the Lord
Lord of all hopefulness, Lord of all joy
Immortal, invisible, God only wise
Angel voices ever singing
Praise to the Holiest in the height
O thou who camest from above
For all the saints

All the above are included in this book, plus a number of others which attracted a good number of votes. Some hymns have been omitted for lack of space but the choice is largely that of the Survey rather than a personal one. This book also had its origins on Lake Como in Italy where for some twelve years (from 1980 to 1992) I was privileged to be summer chaplain at the beautiful Anglican Church of the Ascension at Cadenabbia. Every Sunday night at 9 p.m. we had a 'Songs of Praise' for the many holiday-makers and I told some of the Stories in this book before singing the hymns themselves to the accompaniment of the fine organ in the church there. We welcomed all denominations and also had splendid 'cantica ecumenica' with the local Roman Catholics who proved to be very good at singing many old favourites, both in Italian and English. Back home I have also been able to contribute a monthly Story to about a hundred or so parish magazines and to *The Welsh Churchman*, leading to numerous requests that the Stories be published.

Unfortunately Parkinson's disease has meant a long delay in my doing so, but better late than never, and this has only been possible now due to the unstinted efforts of my dear wife Betty who has done all the typing and borne with me nobly and patiently during the preparation necessary to get the Stories into print. I would also like to place on record my debt of gratitude to the members of my local 'Borderline' study group, of largely retired clergy and lay readers, who helped me in collating the results of my national survey, and my appreciation of the splendid efforts of Peter Clements and the Choir of St Peter's Bexhill with the Meridian TV programme about it. It has been rather difficult for me on the whole but well worth persevering and proved in the end a labour of love.

Abide with me; fast falls the eventide
Praise, my soul, the King of heaven

'ARGUABLY THE MOST FAMILIAR HYMNS IN THE ENGLISH LANGUAGE'

Just behind the *Promenade des Anglais* in the peaceful churchyard of the English Church at Nice is a grave visited constantly by many from all parts of the world, for here lies buried Henry Francis Lyte, who has bequeathed to us two lovely hymns, now universally popular.

He was vicar of the fishing port of Brixham, Devon, on the south coast of England, in the first half of the last century. A remarkable and gifted clergyman of the High-Church persuasion, he was born at Ednam near Kelso, Scotland, on 1 June 1793. Three times he gained the prize in English Poetry at Trinity College, Dublin, where he graduated in 1814. After various curacies he was appointed to Brixham in 1823, where he remained till 1847. He took pupils at the Vicarage to help out with the family finances, amongst them the future illustrious English Foreign Secretary and Prime Minister, Lord Salisbury. At that time the most general form of hymnody was still the metrical versions of the psalms, or hymns based upon them. So it was in 1834 that Lyte first published his *Spirit of the Psalms*, and in this collection Psalm 67 became *God of mercy, God of grace* and Psalm 84 *Pleasant are thy courts above*. The greatest of them all, however, was his fine paraphrase of Psalm 103, *Praise, my soul, the King of heaven*. Indeed, for hymns such as these alone Lyte deserves to be remembered, but one greater and more famous was to follow, although occasioned by profound tragedy.

We are told that Lyte had a special desire 'to leave behind him something that would live to the glory of

God' and in one of his poems entitled 'Declining Days' appears this stanza:

> O Thou! whose touch can lend
> Life to the dead. Thy quickening grace supply
> And grant me swan-like, my last breath to spend
> In song that may not die!

His prayer was to be answered literally, for in 1847 fate struck. Only 54, he contracted the dreaded tuberculosis, for which in those days no cure was known. On Sunday, 5 September, he preached his farewell sermon and assisted at his last Eucharist. Afterwards he retired to his study and an hour or so later emerged with the manuscript of some verses which he entrusted to his daughter. Soon after he left Brixham for ever and set out for the sunnier climate of the Riviera. The journey tired him greatly and when he reached Nice he knew that his end was near. As he lay dying he asked if an Anglican priest could be found to administer the last sacraments. Fortunately there was none other than the Archdeacon of Chichester staying in the same hotel, Henry Edward Manning, later to go over to Rome and become Cardinal Manning of Westminster. 'Heaven's morning' broke for Lyte and he passed away on 20 November 1847.

But why is Lyte's grave so important? What were the verses he handed to his daughter at Brixham? They were the words of one of the most famous hymns ever written, beginning: 'Abide with me; fast falls the eventide' (it is probable that originally he had written it much earlier). It has brought comfort to countless mourners everywhere. It rings round football stadiums as well as great cathedrals and country churches. Some say that it is the most popular hymn in the English language; certainly it is so well known that equally many maintain that it is vastly overdone, mournful and sentimentalized. In reality however it is a glorious affirmation of faith and hope, strong and confident:

I fear no foe, with thee at hand to bless;
Ills have no weight, and tears no bitterness.
Where is death's sting? Where, grave, thy victory?
I triumph still, if thou abide with me.

Tunes have a great deal to do with the popularity of hymns. Lyte had his own melody for the words of *Abide with me*, but is arguable whether the hymn would have become so popular had it not been for the tune 'Eventide', one of the many composed by Dr William Henry Monk, organist at Stoke Newington Church, for the first edition of *Hymns Ancient and Modern* (1861). At a time of great personal sorrow, he had stood and watched the glorious setting sun and so gained the inspiration for his music.

Dame Clara Butt, the contralto singer who died in 1936, made famous her solo setting of the hymn, but it is Monk's 'Eventide' that persists today. The fine tune of *Praise, my soul* was composed in 1869 by Sir John Goss, organist at St Paul's Cathedral and composer to the Chapel Royal.

All Creatures of our God and King

October is the month when Christendom remembers one of its greatest lights of all time, Francis of Assisi, whom God raised up to call the thirteenth-century Church back to a new vision of her mission. From him came that glorious hymn the *Canticle of the Sun*, upon which a number of other hymns have been based. Beethoven wrote his finest music when he could not himself hear a note and Francis praised God for 'our brother the sun who brings us the light' at the very time that he was almost blind and near the end of his life. It was a profound theological truth which enabled this remarkable man so to make his own Benedicite and see in all nature around him the handiwork of his God. To him, earth, sun, moon, stars, fire, wind and water were indeed brothers and sisters, and he could see the natural order infused with the super-natural, a daily miracle for which he could only sing in thankfulness.

The translation I like best is by Matthew Arnold and has been set to a lovely chanting melody by Martin Shaw, which the composer in turn based on the plainsong original. I always find it very moving every time it is sung in church: 'Fair is he, and shining with a very great splendour, O Lord, he signifies to us thee' – so Francis hymns the sun he could no longer see. And I love too the lines towards the end of the canticle: 'Praised be my Lord for all those who pardon one another for his love's sake: and who endure weakness and tribulation.' And the glorious faith and hope which at the close welcome the transition to the 'other side' with such peace and assurance: 'Praised be my Lord for our sister the death of the body, blessed are they who are found walking in thy

8

most holy will.' Francis died soon after he had written this lovely swan-song. It was the night of 3 October 1226. The story has it that as he died 'a multitude of larks came about the roof of the house where he lay and, flying a little way off did make a wheel like a circle round the roof, and by sweet singing did seem to be praising the Lord along with him'.

Another translation that will be familiar to most readers is that by William Henry Draper, who died in 1933. He wrote it for a Whitsuntide festival of school children at Leeds when he was rector of a Yorkshire parish, and it is included in most modern hymnals. Like the original, it avoids sentimentality and is a fine example of good hymn-writing. It is usually sung to the joyful 'Easter Song' – Ralph Vaughan Williams' arrangement of a seventeenth-century melody from Cologne, 'Lasst uns erfreuen', which fits the words admirably.

> All creatures of our God and King,
> Lift up your voice and with us sing
>   Alleluia, Alleluia!
> Thou burning sun with golden beam,
> Thou silver moon with softer gleam,
>   O praise him, O praise him,
>   Alleluia, Alleluia, Alleluia.

All glory, laud and honour

'THE PRISONER'S SONG'

A story is told that on the morning of Palm Sunday, AD 821, in the French town of Angers, in Anjou. It was a very important Palm Sunday for the local citizens, for their King Louis the Pious was coming to worship at their church. But the Bishop of Orleans, whose name was Theodulph, was imprisoned in a monastery nearby, arrested on suspicion of involvement in a conspiracy.

As the King and his entourage approach the church, they halt. He calls for silence and, as all listen, a man's voice can be heard singing very beautifully. The King listens with great attention and then, when it has ceased, he sends his servants to find out who it was and what were the verses he sang so splendidly. He learns that it is in fact the imprisoned Bishop Theodulph and, much moved, orders his immediate release. He also gives orders that Theodulph's song shall be sung every Palm Sunday from then onwards.

And so it has been, for the song was called *Gloria, Laus et Honor* and has become one of the greatest Christian hymns the world over; there are very few churches where it is not sung every Palm Sunday – *All Glory, laud and honour/To thee, Redeemer, King*. The most popular English translation was made last century by Dr John Mason Neale, founder of the East Grinstead Sisters, whom Archbishop Trench described as the most profoundly learned hymnologist of our Church. Other very popular Neale translations which are loved everywhere include *O come, O come, Emmanuel* (see pages 89–90), *Jerusalem the golden*, *O happy band of pilgrims*, and *The day of Resurrection*.

If we sometimes feel that in Neale's translation 'All glory' is a little long, it may be well to remember that originally Bishop Theodulph gave it no less than 39 verses! One verse not sung nowadays contains the line:

Be thou, O Lord, the Rider
And we the little Ass,
That to God's Holy City
Together we may pass.

One of the most vivid memories I shall always treasure is when, as Managing Director of the then Church Pilgrimage Association, I organized the visit to the Holy Land of Dr Donald Coggan, when he was still Archbishop of York and before he moved to Canterbury. We went to the little Church at Bethphage on the far side of the Mount of Olives and processed ourselves up over the top, past the church of Pater Noster, down via the Dominus Flevit to the Garden of Gethsemane, following literally in our Lord's steps on the first Palm Sunday. We all carried fresh palm branches and sang lustily as we made our little procession:

Thou didst accept their praises;
Accept the prayers we bring,
Who in all good delightest,
Thou good and gracious King.

'CROWN HIM LORD OF ALL'

There are some authors and composers remembered today for only one hymn or tune. This is certainly the case with *Crown him Lord of all*, the Ascensiontide hymn *par excellence*. The author was Edward Perronet (1726–1792), a product of the great Evangelical Revival of the eighteenth century. Wesley himself thought highly of him, for he knew very well that to write a good hymn was no easy task and his judgement has been confirmed by the few that have remained from among the vast number written at that time.

All hail the power of Jesu's name first appeared in the *Gospel Magazine* in 1780 and was quickly recognized as a really great hymn. In fact Perronet, son of the Vicar of Sundridge in Kent, like many others of his day, left the Church of England. He annoyed Wesley by publishing a very harsh satire on the Church which he described as 'a tottering edifice which I despise' – shades of today's popular Press. (John and Charles Wesley both remained loyal Anglicans at the time). Perronet then attached himself to a strongly Calvinistic sect known as The Countess of Huntingdon's Connexion. Later still he became an Independent minister at Canterbury, where he died at the age of 66. He had an adventurous life – on one occasion at Bolton he was set upon by a mob and rolled in the mud. At Canterbury he met William Shrubsole, formerly a chorister at the cathedral (and one-time organist at Bangor Cathedral) but likewise now disenchanted with the Established Church. Shrubsole wrote a stirring tune for Perronet's verses called 'Miles Lane', which Elgar said he considered the finest hymn tune in the English heritage. The names of Perronet and Shrubsole are now largely forgotten but their fine hymn remains and retains its affection amongst Christians of all denominations. The Church of England was much kinder in the end than either of its critics, for it allowed Perronet to be buried in Canterbury Cathedral cloisters.

All hail the power of Jesu's name is indeed a great hymn of praise to the risen and ascended Christ (drawing on the imagery of the Book of Revelation) and speaking of 'King of kings and Lord of lords', angels, saints and martyrs and all redeemed creation paying tribute to the Lord of all. The complete wording was subsequently revised in 1787 by Dr John Rippon, a Baptist minister who called it the Christian 'Coronation Hymn of Jesus'. Whilst 'Miles Lane' is indeed an excellent tune, still rightly sung in many of our churches today, many also believe the Welsh have an even finer tune, 'Diadem'.

> Let every tribe and every tongue
> Before him prostrate fall;
> And shout in universal song
> The crownèd Lord of all.

All things bright and beautiful
There is a green hill far away
Once in royal David's city

'THE GODMOTHER'S HYMNS THAT EVERYONE LOVES'

Cecil Frances Alexander died on 12 October 1895. She was a remarkable woman (we must not be misled by the 'Cecil') who has given us not one, but three of our best-known hymns. She was the author of *All things bright and beautiful, There is a green hill far away* and *Once in royal David's city*. In fact, if we accept, as we must, that Christmas, Good Friday and Easter, and the Harvest Thanksgiving are the times when most churches get their largest congregations, then Mrs Alexander makes her contribution, year by year, without fail and there can be few places where her favourites are not sung with great affection.

We can add to the list others, too: for example, *Jesus calls us o'er the tumult* for St Andrewstide, and *I bind unto myself today* (St Patrick's Breastplate), which she translated from the Irish original for St Patrick's Day 1889. Ireland for her was of great importance, for not only was she born in County Wicklow (1818) but she married William Alexander, later to become Bishop of Derry and then Archbishop of Armagh and Primate of the Church of Ireland. She was a prolific writer and produced over four hundred hymns altogether, most of them for children. Her *Hymns for Little Children* (1848) subsequently ran to more than a hundred editions.

It is said that she began writing these hymns after hearing one of her godchildren complaining that he found difficulty in understanding the catechism. So to make it more interesting she began composing some verses to illustrate the principal doctrines of the creed; in this context the three 'favourites' already cited quickly fall into place. In *Essays Catholic and Critical*, Dr N. P. Williams chose *There is a green hill* as the basis for his exposition of the doctrine of the atonement, so eloquent is it in both its orthodoxy and simplicity.

It is believed that when writing *There is a green hill* Mrs Alexander had in mind a small grass-covered hill just outside the walls of Londonderry which reminded her of Calvary, though she never actually visited Jerusalem itself to see the site of the crucifixion. 'Without a city wall' is somewhat confusing, especially for children, and many hymnals alter it to 'outside a city wall'.

Altered too is the rendering of *All things bright and beautiful*, for times have changed and there can be few, if any, churches now that retain the lines

> The rich man in his castle,
>   The poor man at his gate,
> God made them high and lowly,
>   And ordered their estate.

Mrs Alexander was obviously governed by the social mores of her time but in fairness we should point out that the catechism does not say 'to do my duty in that state of life unto which it *has* pleased God to call me' but 'it *shall* please God'. It is a delightful and fine hymn none the less, with obvious Franciscan connotations which are very appropriate since St Francis' Day is 4 October, the time of Harvest Thanksgivings galore.

Once in royal David's city is one of the best-loved Christmas hymns. Many believe that Christmas really begins when the lovely solo choirboy's voice sings out the first verse from King's College Chapel at Cambridge on the memorable Christmas Eve broadcast of the *Nine Lessons and Carols*.

As always, tunes are important. There is no dispute at all about H. Gauntlet's 'Irby' for *Once in royal David's city*, or W. Horsley's 'Horsley' for *There is a green hill far away*, but for her hymn on creation, Martin Shaw's adaptation of the English traditional melody 'Royal Oak' is now popular with the younger generation, whereas W. H. Monk's 'All things bright and beautiful' still holds sway amongst the oldies.

We can all thank God for Mrs Alexander's wonderful gift whatever the tune. She was certainly greatly loved by all who came into contact with her. She worked much with the poor and needy and the profits she received from her writings all went to an Irish school for children with speech impairments.

And did those feet in ancient time

'JERUSALEM'

Far ahead of his time, a poet, a prophet and a mystic, William Blake was a remarkable man by any assessment and it is from his preface to *Milton*, written and etched in 1804, that we get the verses which have become, since World War I, so popular as a hymn. King George V is said to have wanted the lines adopted as a national anthem and the Women's Institutes have already made it theirs, whilst it was rung out regularly from school assemblies and even Labour Party meetings.

It was Robert Bridges who suggested (in 1916) to Sir Hubert Parry that these words of Blake should be set to music and they were first sung as part of a music festival in the Albert Hall, where they are still rendered with characteristic enthusiasm by the last night Promenaders. The words and music make an impressive harmony and it is not surprising they have become so popular. Some theologians are unhappy at the Pelagianism (do-it-yourself philosophy) that would build 'Jerusalem in England's green and pleasant land' and they no doubt have a point. But in their context, and in Blake's own belief, they are surely profoundly Christian in the best and fullest sense. The eternal was, for him, not just a hoped-for 'hereafter' but a reality for now and always.

Blake began his artist's life with half-a-crown, married a market gardener's daughter and died virtually unknown to be buried in a pauper's grave. He had led a life given over to genuine spirituality like St Teresa of Avila, who was his greatest source of inspiration. 'He knew the way to the mountains. He could pass with natural ease to and fro between this world and the next. He entered in and saw the secrets of the land unknown.' (Source unknown.) It was because of this that Blake was so

17

concerned with the problems of his time – the 'dark satanic mills' of the Industrial Revolution and the materialism it brought. 'Desire of gain,' he wrote, 'deadens the genius of man. My business is not to gather gold but to make glorious shapes, expressing God-like sentiments.'

He died as he had lived. He prophesied that 'the bells of Heaven would ring and the trumpets sound' to welcome him and he believed it with all his being. 'I cannot think of death as any more than going from one room to another.' As he lay dying he turned to his wife: 'Kate,' he said, 'I will draw your portrait.' And having drawn her he burst out with cries of 'Alleluia' and then his spirit, we are told, departed 'like the sighing of a gentle breeze' on 11 August in 1827, when he was in his seventieth year.

And now, O Father, mindful of the love
Once, only once, and once for all

'THE HYMNS OF THE
"DON FROM DONCASTER" '

More than a generation ago when I was editing *Church Illustrated*, *Anglican World* and *Sunday* magazines, my good friend Richard Tatlock, then on the staff of the Religious Department of the BBC, instigated a poll, asking readers to name their Top Ten favourite hymns. I well remember that the postman had to work overtime and that we were inundated with thousands of entries from all parts of the UK, and indeed overseas as well. We all had our own ideas as to which would be the overall winner. It was not *Abide with me* (4th), *The King of love* (5th), nor *Praise my soul, the King of heaven* (8th). Of course, *The day thou gavest, For all the saints, Lead, kindly light*, and Blake's *Jerusalem* all had their firm supporters at that time. But far and away most popular with all ages, in the number one place, came a famous Communion hymn written by an Oxford professor of the last century, William Bright, beginning with the words: 'And now, O Father, mindful of the love/That bought us, once for all, on Calvary's tree'.

William Bright was born in 1824. After being tutored by the great Dr Thomas Arnold of Rugby, he went up to Oxford and eventually became Regius Professor of Church History at the University, earning the nickname of the 'Don from Doncaster', where he was born. A staunch Tractarian, like many others at the time he suffered persecution for his (allegedly) 'popish' beliefs. Nevertheless, when the first edition of *Hymns Ancient and Modern* was produced in 1861 there were no fewer than ten of his hymns in it.

He was also an eminent liturgical authority and in 1857 published his scholarly work, *The Ancient Collects*, which was later to form the basis for the revision of the *Book of Common Prayer* in the 1928 revised Prayer Book. Some maintained that Bright was the only person since Cranmer who could really write a good English collect. To return to his hymn, Bright's words provide a powerful 'musical prayer' for us all, whatever our tradition of churchmanship:

> Look, Father, look on his anointed face,
>   And only look on us as found in him;
> Look not on our misusings of thy grace,
>   Our prayer so languid, and our faith so dim;
> For lo, between our sins and their reward
> We set the Passion of thy Son our Lord.
>
> And then for those, our dearest and our best,
>   By this prevailing presence we appeal;
> O fold them closer to thy mercy's breast,
>   O do Thine utmost for their souls' true weal.

In the 1950s it topped the poll, whereas in my survey in 1995 it came 54th. Bright's words are a paraphrase from the Oblation in the Canon in the Latin Mass beginning 'Unde et Memores', first published in *The Eucharistic Presentation* by Bright in 1873. The tune is also similarly named and was written by Dr Monk (composer also of 'Eventide' and many other favourites) for the revised edition of *Hymns Ancient and Modern* in 1875.

Bright was also the author of *Once, only once, and once for all*, based on 1 Corinthians 11.26, 'As often as you eat this bread and drink the cup, you proclaim the Lord's death until he comes', first published in *Hymns and Other Poems* in 1866. The tune of 'Albano' first appeared in the Appendix of *Hymns Ancient and Modern* (1868) 'from composer's original manuscript'.

His manhood pleads where now it lives
    On heaven's eternal throne,
And where in mystic rite he gives
    Its Presence to his own.

And so we show thy death, O Lord,
    Till thou again appear;
And feel, when we approach thy board,
    We have an altar here.

Angel voices, ever singing

'DEDICATING A NEW ORGAN'

This hymn was written for a very particular occasion: the dedication in 1861 of the new organ in Wingate Church, Lancashire, where the Vicar, whose name was Macrorie (later a bishop in South Africa), had invited his friend – Francis Pott – to write a new hymn in honour of the great event. Francis Pott (ordained 1857) served curacies in Bishopsworth in Somerset and at both Ardingly and Ticehurst in Sussex, before becoming Rector of Northill, Bedfordshire, in 1866. After ministering there for some 25 years, deafness and general ill health compelled his retirement, though he did not remain idle and spent his time translating into really lovely English many of the ancient Latin and Greek hymns, including *Forty days and forty nights* and *The strife is o'er, the battle done*. His 'organ dedication' hymn at Wingate undoubtedly comprises his best and well-known original verses and begins: 'Angel voices, ever singing/Round thy throne of light'. The third verse, beginning: 'Yea, we know that thou rejoicest/O'er each work of thine', ends with the well-known words – obviously referring to the new organ – 'Craftsman's art and music's measure/For thy pleasure/All combine'. The author is obviously reminding us also that when we worship in church it is with 'hearts and minds and hands and voices' that we produce the 'choicest Psalmody'.

Francis Pott was also an expert on liturgy and High Churchman of his time, a member of the committee that compiled the first edition of *Hymns Ancient and Modern*. The new hymnal was accused by many of being 'popish', an allegation which nowadays sounds absurd.

The tune for *Angel voices* was written especially to fit the words by the Victorian organist and hymn composer Dr E. G. Monk.

At all events, we can still, one and a half centuries later, sing with confidence Francis Pott's lovely words:

> Can it be that thou regardest
>   Songs of sinful man?
> Can we know that thou art near us
>   And wilt hear us?
>   Yea - we can.

As with gladness men of old
Alleluia! sing to Jesus
To thee, O Lord, our hearts we raise

'THREE FAMOUS HYMNS FROM BRISTOL'

Some 140 years ago a shipping agent in Bristol was unwell and unable to go to church on the Feast of the Epiphany (6 January), as otherwise he certainly would have done, for he was a devout Tractarian (a member of the High-Church Oxford Movement) and became a well-known hymn-writer of his day. So he read the Gospel for the day from his Book of Common Prayer (Matthew 2.1–12) recording the age-old story of the Magi finding their way to the infant Jesus at Bethlehem. As he meditated he came to see that the 'wise men' were examples for all Christians to follow in their search for truth. Thus from his sick bed he put his ideas into verse, and so was born one of the most popular Epiphany hymns.

The writer's name was William Chatterton Dix and he lived from 1837 to 1898. The hymn he wrote on 6 January 1860 is the much-loved:

> As with gladness men of old,
> Did the guiding star behold,
> As with joy they hailed its light,
> Leading onwards, beaming bright;
> So, most gracious Lord, may we
> Evermore be led to thee.

The tune to which the hymn is sung everywhere actually carries the name 'Dix' and was composed in 1838 by the German composer Conrad Kocher. Dix himself said he was not very fond of it but majority opinion has not shared his dislike and it has become a great favourite.

In 1867 Dix published his *Altar Songs* and amongst

these was another hymn which has since become justly popular: *Alleluia! sing to Jesus*, which he intended first and foremost as a eucharistic hymn.

> Though the cloud from sight received him
>   When the forty days were o'er,
> Shall our hearts forget his promise,
>   'I am with you evermore'?

This is almost always sung these days to the fine Welsh tune 'Hyfrydol' by Rowland Huw Pritchard. Tunes always affect the popularity of hymns and this is equally true of Dix's well-known Harvest hymn *To Thee, O Lord, our hearts we raise* which was set to music by the great Sir Arthur Sullivan ('Golden Sheaves').

So all in all we have much cause to thank God for William Chatterton Dix and sing his hymns with renewed understanding and appreciation.

At the name of Jesus

'KING OF GLORY' FROM ROMSEY ABBEY

The lovely Abbey Church of Romsey in Hampshire makes a magnificent witness to our Christian heritage. Today, as throughout the long centuries since our Norman ancestors first built it, the massive pillars speak of strength and firm foundations. It can come, therefore, as no real surprise to learn that it was Romsey that gave birth to a great hymn of thanksgiving and hope in the victory of the risen and ascended Christ –

> At the Name of Jesus
> Every knee shall bow,
> Every tongue confess him
> King of glory now.

But it is therefore quite a considerable surprise to learn that this powerful hymn in fact comes to us from a woman invalid in a wheelchair, and was one of a collection of hymns published (in 1861) under the title *Verses for the Sick and Lonely*. The author was Caroline Noel and her address the Vicarage of Romsey, for she was the daughter of the then Vicar, the Hon. Gerald Noel. Caroline was born just after the Battle of Waterloo and died 60 years later in 1877, but she remained an invalid all her life. *At the name of Jesus* is based of course on the opening verses of Philippians 2 and is essentially triumphalist in its vision of the whole world subject to Christ, its King.

In contrast to the view held by many nowadays that one religion is as true as another, and that it is arrogant for us as Christians to try to convert, for example, Muslims or Jews. Carried to its logical extreme this argument would have prohibited Augustine or any of the other missionaries from bringing the gospel to our own shores and we would still be 'pagan' as Druids, or worshipping the Norse gods of the Vikings. Caroline Noel preferred the biblical imperative:

> For all wreaths of empire
> Meet upon his brow,
> And our hearts confess him
> King of glory now.

As to the tune, it is usually sung to the much-loved 'Evelyns' of Dr W. H. Monk. He died in 1889 just after he had passed for press the final proofs of the supplement to the second edition of *Hymns Ancient and Modern*, having been musical editor since the hymnal's inception. 'Evelyns' is a good marriage of words and music and it is the tune chosen in both the *New English Hymnal* and the New Standard version of *Hymns Ancient and Modern*. Although the majority of church congregations have been brought up with 'Evelyns', it is increasingly replaced nowadays by the much more modern 'Camberwell' by Michael Brierley. Whichever tune is used, Caroline Noel's words are still magnificent:

> Name him, brothers, name him
> With love as strong as death,
> But with awe and wonder
> And with bated breath.
> He is God the Saviour,
> He is Christ the Lord,
> Ever to be worshipped,
> Trusted and adored.

Be thou my vision, O Lord of my heart

'OUR CELTIC INHERITANCE'

One of the glories of Ireland is its great heritage of Celtic culture, especially in Christian art and literature. The recent revival of interest in Celtic spirituality and forms of worship has led to a renewed appreciation of this culture. The *Irish Church Hymnal* in 1919 contained an English translation of an eighth-century poem, 'Rob tu mo bhoile' ('Be thou my vision'), which then spread to other parts of Christendom. It appears in both the *New English Hymnal* and the New Standard edition of *Hymns Ancient and Modern*. The translation was by Mary Byrne, a great authority on the Celtic tradition, and was made into a hymn by Dr Eleanor Hull and included in her *Poem Book in the Gael*. Not surprisingly it caught on fairly quickly with church congregations, sung to the lovely old Irish folk melody 'Slane', which Dr Percy Dearmer also had in mind when he asked Joyce Placzek (see page 80) of Rye in East Sussex to contribute her 'All Day' hymn – *Lord of all hopefulness, Lord of all joy* – to the enlarged edition of his new hymnal called *Songs of Praise*, published by the Oxford University Press in 1931. In both hymns, words and music are well matched. The words of *Be thou my vision* are certainly superb:

> Riches I heed not, nor man's empty praise,
> Be thou mine inheritance now and always;
> Be thou and thou only the first in my heart;
> O Sovereign of heaven, my treasure thou art.

> High King of heaven, thou heaven's bright Sun,
> O grant me its joys, after vict'ry is won;
> Great Heart of my own heart, whatever befall,
> Still be thou my vision, O Ruler of all.

Christians, awake, salute the happy morn

'A CHRISTMAS PRESENT FOR DOLLY'

It is strange how things happen; for instance, how many of us know that we owe one of our most popular Christmastide hymns to a little girl's request that her father should give her a rather unusual Christmas present, a poem written especially for her? Yet this is exactly what happened in Manchester one Christmastide over two centuries ago. The child's name was Dolly and her father was John Byrom. He was a scholar of some note, a Fellow of Trinity College and of the Royal Society. He was also a Jacobite (a supporter of the Stuart kings), not a very safe cause so soon after the '45 rebellion led by Bonnie Prince Charlie, but one which presupposed firm adherence to his outlook and conviction to uphold the orthodox faith as held by Charles I and Archbishop Laud.

So, when on that Christmas morning of 1749 Dolly came down to breakfast, she found at her place a scroll tied in red ribbon and inscribed 'Christmas Day – for Dolly'. She was delighed with 'her' poem, which began: 'Christians, awake, salute the happy morn/Whereon the Saviour of the world was born'. Soon Dolly's poem became quite widely known and John Wainwright, the organist at Stockport Parish Church, decided it would make a fine hymn, so set to providing a suitable tune to fit Byrom's words. This he did with great success, calling his tune 'Yorkshire', and we still sing it with great gusto today! A year later – on Christmas Day, 1750 – Dolly and her father were awakened by singing beneath their windows, and, sure enough, raising their voices lustily below were Mr Wainwright and his choir urging them both to 'Rise to adore the mystery of love which hosts of angels chanted from above'.

Whether in a little country church or in a great cathedral, or carol singing in the street, Christians of all denominations have followed the same advice and sung out the gospel, the good news of Christ's birth, year by year. Byrom wrote his verses in two parts. The first four stanzas faithfully relate the nativity story as in Luke 2.8–20. The second part bids us to remember and 'ponder in our mind God's wondrous love in saving lost mankind'. It is sound advice we all need in each generation:

> Trace we the Babe, who hath retrieved our loss,
> From his poor manger to his bitter cross;
> Then may we hope, angelic hosts among,
> To sing, redeemed, a glad triumphal song.

We hear a great deal about the materialism of our society today and the commercialization of Christmas. Dolly's present from her father went right to the heart of the matter and we can all share in their happiness and joy.

Christ is made the sure foundation
(Blessed City, heavenly Salem)

'THE HEAVENLY ARCHITECT'

An ancient Office hymn (and for my money one of the most beautiful) is *Urbs beata – Blessed City, heavenly Salem* and this is the proper hymn for the Dedication Festival of one's church. Since the actual date of dedication is not known for the majority of our more ancient buildings the usual custom is that the Festival is observed on the first Sunday in October.

> Many a blow and biting sculpture
> Polished well those stones elect,
> In their places now compacted
> By the heavenly Architect,
> Who therewith hath willed for ever
> That his palace should be decked.

The picture of the 'Heavenly Jerusalem' in all its perfection contrasted inevitably with the imperfections of the earthly one in the sense of the 'temples made with hands' has always been an important theme of Christian hymnody. We can go back at least to the seventh century (some would believe even earlier) for the lovely words of *Urbs beata*. It is in two parts (one for Matins and one for Evensong) and the second part, beginning 'Christ is made the sure foundation', is nowadays probably more widely known than the first. The translation in almost all hymn books is that of our old friend, John Mason Neale. And although he took quite a few liberties with the Latin the result is very satisfying. Another translation of the second part of the hymn is John Chandler's *Christ is our corner-stone*, particularly loved it would be fair to say by Anglicans of the generation now usually referred to as 'senior citizens'. It is set to Samuel Sebastian Wesley's

31

fine tune 'Harewood'. The tunes are as fine as the words. Nothing can possibly equal the majesty of the plainsong (the Sarum mode is printed in most of our hymn books) but three modern tunes are all popular: 'Oriel' from the *Cantica Sacra* of 1840; Henry Edward Hodson's 'Urbs Coelestis' (English Hymnal) and, especially nowadays it seems, 'Westminster Abbey', which is an arrangement by Ernest Hawkins of the *Alleluias* at the end of Henry Purcell's anthem *O God, Thou art my God*. It's a splendid hymn to sing anyway, whether your tune be ancient or modern. And the Roman Catholic *Parish Hymn Book* rightly reminds us that what we are singing here is based on Paul's Letter to the Ephesians in which he pictures the Church made of living stones with Jesus as the 'head' (Ephesians 2.19–22).

> Christ is made the sure foundation,
> Christ the head and corner-stone,
> Chosen of the Lord, and precious,
> Binding all the Church in one,
> Holy Sion's help for ever,
> And her confidence alone.

Come, ye thankful people, come

'THE GOOD DEAN'S "THANK YOU" HYMN'

This popular Harvest hymn is over 150 years old and was written by Dean Henry Alford of Canterbury, a devout man and a great scholar, if somewhat eccentric (as a young man he wrote love letters to his betrothed in the form of a Greek grammar!). Much earlier, at the tender age of only six, he had written *The Travels of St Paul* and when still only eleven he published a *Collection of Hymns for Sundry Occasions*. Later on he was to edit *The Contemporary Review*, a periodical covering religious, political and literary subjects of the time.

At first, Alford's famous *Come, ye thankful people, come* had some seven eight-lined verses but now only four of them are usually sung. And with modern farming methods it is a bit difficult to find any season in the year when we can genuinely sing 'All is safely gathered in', but nonetheless the Dean's words are eloquent in summing up the message of the harvest in a meaningful way, both for here and now and for the Final Judgement: 'Let thy saints be gathered in,/Free from sorrow, free from sin.'

The one (and only) tune, 'St George', was composed by Sir George Elvey, organist at St George's Chapel, Windsor, who also gave us the popular 'Diademata' for *Crown him with many crowns*. 'St George' is sometimes sung also to Jane Leeson's *Christ the Lord is risen again*, but such is its 'harvest' association that it somehow seems odd now to sing it at any other time.

Dean Alford also wrote the lovely All Saintstide hymn *Ten thousand times ten thousand*, very popular at the time, and when I was a choirboy, but seldom heard now. It is such a joyful hymn when faced with the inevitability of death and the life to come. The same theme of glorious hope is evidenced by Alford's own tombstone in St

Martin's churchyard at Canterbury, where the inscription reads 'Deversorium viatoris proficientis Hierosolymam' – 'The inn of a pilgrim travelling to Jerusalem'. Let us remember that splendid epitaph whenever we sing the good Dean's hymn (as revised by the compilers of *Hymns Ancient and Modern*).

> Come, then, Lord of mercy, come,
> Bid us sing thy harvest-home;
> Let thy saints be gathered in,
> Free from sorrow, free from sin.
> All upon the golden floor,
> Praising thee for evermore;
> Come, with all thine angels, come,
> Bid us sing thy harvest-home.

Dear Lord and Father of mankind
Immortal love for ever full

'THE HYMNS THAT WERE NEVER INTENDED!'

One of the most popular hymns today is, strangely enough, *Dear Lord and Father of mankind*. I say 'strangely enough' for it was never intended as a hymn in the first place! This is because it is Quaker in origin, and the Society of Friends do not usually sing hymns at all in their worship. In fact, the author, John Greenleaf Whittier, always maintained that he knew nothing about music and was certainly not a hymn-writer but a mystical poet. Nonetheless, and not surprisingly, some of his fine verses were soon included in various hymnals and as time went on they have found their way into compilations of many different churches and denominations worldwide.

Whittier was born in 1807 in Haverhill, Massachusetts, USA, where he spent his whole life. His father was a successful farmer and wanted John to follow him on the land. John, however, had other ideas and turned to journalism and poetry, for which he had an undoubted gift. He became editor of the *Pennsylvania Freeman*, a paper dedicated to the movement for the abolition of slavery, a cause to which John was totally committed. He wore the special dress of the Society of Friends all his life, which spanned pretty well the whole of the nineteenth century and ended on 7 September 1892.

Dear Lord and Father of mankind was part of a poem, *The Brewing of Soma*, which Whittier wrote in 1872. Soma was a potent drink made by the Indians to produce a state of frenzy and this was one of the 'foolish ways' of which the poem speaks – the 'still small voice of calm' replacing the 'heat of our desire'. We are reminded of the call of the first disciples in Galilee, rather oddly described as the 'Syrian sea'; the New Testament knows the 'Sea of Galilee', 'the Lake of Gennesaret' and 'the Sea of Tiberias' but no 'Syrian sea'.

Sir Hubert Parry's tune 'Repton', from his oratorio *Judith* (1888), is partly responsible for the popularity of the hymn today. It fits Whittier's words most eloquently, as if written especially to complement them. In the same way the fine tune 'Bishopsthorpe', composed by Jeremiah Clarke of 'Trumpet Voluntary' fame (1673–1707; the organist at both St Paul's Cathedral and the Chapel Royal), is just right for the other great hymn for which we have to thank our Quaker poet, this time from his verses entitled *Our Master*, published in 1867. *Immortal love for ever full* is also justly popular and has comforted many by its simplicity and eloquence.

> Through him the first fond prayers are said,
>   Our lips of childhood frame;
> The last low whispers of our dead
>   are burdened with his name

and

> To turn aside from thee is hell,
>   To walk with thee is heaven.

So the mystical poet's verses are now firm favourites everywhere, and part of our rich heritage of hymnody, without which we woumd be sadly impoverished. *Dear Lord and Father of mankind* was far and away the top favourite in my survey.

Eternal Father, strong to save

'FOR THOSE IN PERIL ON THE SEA'

Many churches observe 'Sea Sunday' in July, when no doubt the seafaring hymn *par excellence* is sung. It is one of everybody's favourites and dates from the publication of the first edition of *Hymns Ancient and Modern* (1861), when the Tractarian Movement was at its height. The author was William Whiting (born 1825), son of a Kensington grocer. Although he was born with a club foot, which inevitably affected his life in many ways, it did not deter him from scholastic excellence at Oxford and at Winchester.

He became Master of the Winchester choirboys (called 'Quiristers'), in charge of their residential home – sixteen brown-liveried boys who were to sing services in the Cathedral and wait on the College Scholars in Hall. Samuel Sebastian Wesley (grandson of Charles Wesley) was appointed organist at Winchester in 1849 and he and Whiting made a formidable team in raising the standard of music in the Cathedral.

Whiting himself had a great interest in poetry and in 1860 submitted to Sir Henry Baker (author of *We love the place, O God* and *The King of love my Shepherd is*) some verses eventually to be sung all over the world: *Eternal Father, strong to save*. Surprising though it may seem, we are told Whiting originally intended this hymn to be treated metaphorically for the sacrament of Baptism, where we all launched onto 'the waves of this trouble-some world'. In fact it was, from the first, interpreted much more literally as a sailor's hymn. He translated it into French: *Pour ceux en peril sur les flots*.

Whiting became increasingly troubled with his club foot and suffered great pain. He died eventually in 1878, but will always be remembered for his famous hymn. The hymn became almost a by-word in Victorian England generally and produced many sentimental pictures. In the Second World War, when Churchill and Roosevelt were at sea, it was sung aboard the battleship HMS *Prince of Wales*.

The tune 'Melita' is also much loved and helped to popularize the hymn. It was composed by John Bacchus Dykes, organist of Durham Cathedral, who died in Ticehurst, Sussex, in 1876. He wrote it specially for the first edition of *Hymns Ancient and Modern* and chose its name appropriately after Malta where St Paul was shipwrecked (Acts 27). So we are indebted both to William Whiting and Bacchus Dykes for this fine sailor's hymn, and since we have always been a sea-faring nation, it is not surprising that it has become such a favourite.

Fight the good fight with all thy might
O worship the Lord in the beauty of holiness

'FAITHFUL SOLDIERS AND SERVANTS'

The theme of Christians being soldiers in Christ's 'army' is deeply rooted both in the New Testament and church tradition. St Paul's familiar passage in Ephesians to 'put on the whole armour of God' is an obvious example and the same emphasis is found in the Book of Common Prayer Baptism Service where at the font we are pledged to be 'Christ's faithful soldiers and servants unto our life's end'. Great organizations such as the Salvation Army and the Church Army clearly demonstrate the same concept and not surprisingly many hymn-writers have taken up the theme and adopted the martial idiom. We have only to quote one or two familiar favourites to realize how true this is, for example, *Onward Christian soldiers, Stand up, stand up, for Jesus* and *Soldiers of Christ arise*. The one which everyone knows and loves is, of course, *Fight the good fight with all thy might*. The author was John Monsell, Rector of St Nicholas at Guildford. He also gave us the fine Epiphanytide hymn *O worship the Lord in the beauty of holiness*, to which we shall refer a little later.

When I was an army padre my Colonel (son of an Australian vicar) insisted we always sang *Fight the good fight* to the old tune 'Pentecost' by Jamaican-born William Boyd. Today most churches sing it to 'Duke Street' by Lancashire-born John Hatton. (By a strange coincidence this tune was included in a collection compiled by William Boyd, who used it for *Veni Creator – Come, Holy Ghost, our souls inspire –* at the specific request of Sabine Baring-Gould, author of *Onward Christian soldiers*).

But to return to John Monsell who, in his preface to

Hymns of Love and Praise (1862), wrote: 'Most of us are too distant and reserved – we sing not as if our hearts were on fire with the divine flame of love and joy as we should hymn Him who is chief in the courts of heaven and altogether lovely.' Monsell met his death due to a tragic accident during roof repairs at St Nicholas. It is all the more poignant since in order to raise funds for the repair work he had written a special poem which began:

> Dear body thou and I must part
> Thy busy head, thy throbbing heart
> Must cease to work, must cease to play
> For me at no far distant day.

Whether or not he had a premonition of death we shall never know, but on the morning of 9 April, 1875, he met with a fatal accident while inspecting the roof repairs. Yet he still speaks to us through his hymns:

> Run the straight race through God's good grace,
> Lift up thine eyes and seek his face;
> Life with its way before us lies,
> Christ is the path, and Christ the prize.
>
> Cast care aside, lean on thy Guide;
> His boundless mercy will provide;
> Trust and thy trusting soul shall prove
> Christ is its life and Christ its love.

Monsell's other great hymn, *O worship the Lord in the beauty of holiness*, has also become justly popular throughout the Christian world:

> Low at his feet lay thy burden of carefulness,
>   High on his heart he will bear it for thee,
> Comfort thy sorrows and answer thy prayerfulness,
>   Guiding thy steps as may best for thee be.
>
> Fear not to enter his courts in the slenderness
>   Of the poor wealth thou would'st reckon as thine;

Truth in its beauty, and love in its tenderness,
    These are the offerings to lay on his shrine.

The hymn is almost always sung to an old German melody of the eighteenth century called 'Was Lebet', which is attributed to Johann Reinhardt in 1754 and fits the words most admirably.

O worship the Lord in the beauty of holiness,
    Bow down before him, his glory proclaim;
With gold of obedience, and incense of lowliness,
    Kneel and adore him, the Lord is his name.

For all the saints who from their labours rest

'THE FELLOWSHIP DIVINE'

He started his ministry as a curate in Kidderminster in 1846 and then was a country vicar in Shropshire for 22 years, before moving to London, as Rector of St Andrew's Undershaft and Bishop of East London (today he would be called Bishop of Stepney but then was designated Bishop of Bedford!). Finally, in 1888 he became Bishop of the newly formed Diocese of Wakefield and was much loved in that northern and heavily industrialized part of the country until he died eleven years later at the age of 74. His name was William Walsham How.

It was in 1864, while he was in Whittington in Shropshire, that he wrote the hymn which sums up in a moving and eloquent way our whole Christian belief in the 'communion of saints': 'O blest communion, fellowship divine!/We feebly struggle, they in glory shine'.

Walsham How did much splendid work and was so loved by the East Enders that he was nicknamed the 'Omnibus Bishop' since he went everywhere by bus at a time when the penny fare was enough for quite long journeys. His wonderful hymn *For all the saints who from their labours rest* is indeed 'omnibus' also, not only because it is now sung in so many different countries and languages but because it expresses so vividly the 'one communion and fellowship' of all those who, as the Book of Common Prayer so aptly describes it, are 'knit together' in Christ their Lord – 'Yet all are one in thee, for all are thine'.

The good Bishop reminds us both of the 'rest' of the faithful warriors after hard-won fight and of the great triumphal song of the multitude which none can number, pouring in from 'earth's wide bounds and ocean's farthest coast'.

When Dr Ralph Vaughan Williams wrote the stirring tune which is sung universally to Bishop How's words, he called it 'Sine Nomine' – 'without name'. Nothing could be more apposite for All Hallows, when we commemorate so many who have no memorial otherwise in the Christian Calendar. But these 'were merciful men whose righteousness has not been forgotten. Their bodies are buried in peace but their name liveth for evermore' (Ecclesiasticus 44.10,14).

For the beauty of the earth

'THE SACRIFICE OF PRAISE'

Folliott Sandford Pierpoint (born 1836; died 1917) was a West Countryman and a well-known classical scholar. He was also a very devoted High Churchman or Tractarian (as followers of the Oxford Movement were more commonly known in his day). In 1864 he was closely associated with the publication of a collection of hymns called *Lyra Eucharistica*, which included his lovely hymn, *For the beauty of the earth*, said to have been inspired by the view he saw from the hillside outside Bath, where he was born and went to school, before going up to Cambridge, where he graduated in 1857. Pierpoint was subsequently ordained into the Anglican Ministry and spent the greater part of his life as classics master at Somerset College. He wrote several books of hymns and poems, including *The Hymnal Noted*, in which he included all the proper Office hymns for the Canonical Hours, the ancient daily services of the monastic orders.

Each verse of *For the beauty of the earth* ended with the refrain 'Christ our God to Thee we raise/This our sacrifice of praise'. The phrase was taken directly from the Book of Common Prayer Communion Service, 'Prayer of Oblation', which says: 'We thy humble servants entirely desire thy fatherly goodness mercifully to accept this our sacrifice of praise and thanksgiving'. He intended the hymn to be sung at the Offertory of the bread and wine for the eucharistic sacrifice. This view of the Eucharist was not accepted by the editors of many other hymnals and so this is why they changed the words to read 'grateful hymn' instead of 'sacrifice'. Understandably the hymn has become very popular indeed at flower festivals and Harvest thanksgivings, both in churches and in schools. Not only does it remind us of God's great gifts in creation (tree and flower, sun and moon, and so on) but also of the human love of family and friends, and, in the author's own version, 'Thy Bride which evermore lifteth holy hands above' – again changed in many hymnals to read 'Church' instead of 'Bride'. (For the original text, see the *English Hymnal* – the old standard book, not the *New English Hymnal*.) He goes on to include 'Martyrs, Prophets and Confessors, Virgins' and 'Thy Maiden mother mild' in the last of eight verses in all, reduced to six in most hymnals.

Without getting too involved in the doctrinal argument about eucharistic sacrifice, we can all find in Pierpoint's words an opportunity to give thanks for so much we all take for granted: our love of countryside, our holidays, the lakes and mountains, and much besides, which inspire everyone to thank their Creator.

> For the beauty of each hour
> Of the day and of the night,
> Hill and vale, and tree and flower,
> Sun and moon and stars of light . . .
>
> For the joy of human love,
> Brother, sister, parent, child,
> Friends on earth and friends above,
> For all gentle thoughts and mild . . .
>
> For each perfect gift of thine
> To our race so freely given,
> Graces human and divine,
> Flowers of earth and buds of heaven.

Different hymnals set different tunes for this great hymn but both 'Dix' – Conrad Kocher's fine tune (see page 24) and 'England's Lane' – Geoffrey Shaw's adaptation of an English folk melody, go admirably with the words.

'SOLID JOYS AND LASTING TREASURE'

The story of how a one-time atheist and slave-trader came to write some of our best-loved hymns is indeed a fascinating one. John Newton, born in London in 1725, went to sea when he was scarcely eleven and at the age of 17 he was press-ganged into the Navy, from which he later deserted; he was captured and publicly flogged. He took to slave-trading and led a dissolute and godless life for many years before undergoing a reawakening in a terrible storm at sea and reading the great classic *The Imitation of Christ* by St Thomas à Kempis. He spent nine years in study before being ordained in 1764 and becoming Curate of Olney in Buckinghamshire. There he became closely associated with the poet William Cowper, which resulted in the publication in 1779 of *The Olney Hymns*, containing 68 hymns by Cowper and some 280 by Newton himself. Amongst the latter were several destined to become lasting favourites: *How sweet the name of Jesus sounds* and *Glorious things of thee are spoken*.

Newton went on to become Rector of St Mary, Woolnoth, in the City of London, where he drew great crowds. He was greatly influenced by John Wesley and George Whitefield, two of the great leaders of the Evangelical Revival in England. John Newton continued to preach until past the age of 80, despite failing eyesight. His faithful servant stood behind him in the pulpit and traced out the lines for him in his manuscript. On one occasion he spoke the words 'Jesus is precious' and then repeated them. His servant whispered to him: 'You've said that already – move on', but Newton's reply was typical of him. He cried out as loud as he could a third time: 'Jesus is precious.' He was greatly loved by his congregation. The historian Thomas Lacey described him as 'one of the purest and most unselfish of men'. He died in 1807, having written his own epitaph: 'John Newton, Clerk: Once an infidel and libertine, A servant of slaves in Africa: Was by the mercy of our Lord and Saviour Jesus Christ, Preserved, restored, pardoned, And appointed to preach the Faith he had so Long laboured to destroy.'

Glorious things was for many years sung to 'Austria', the tune by Joseph Haydn which formed the Austrian and German national anthem. The Emperor 'Kaiser Bill' was considerably surprised when his godmother Queen Victoria, at Windsor, wanted Newton's famous hymn sung to this music at the morning service. Another more modern tune, 'Abbot's Leigh', was written especially for this hymn in 1941 by Cyril Taylor, Head of Religious Broadcasting at the BBC from 1939 to 1958 and editor of *The BBC Hymn Book*.

God be in my head and in my understanding

'A PRAYER FROM SARUM' (1514)

English Christianity owes a great deal to the heritage of Sarum – the old name for Salisbury. It was from the Sarum Liturgy that Archbishop Cranmer drew mainly for the Book of Common Prayer and it was from the *Sarum Primer*, printed by Pynson on 12 May 1514, that we find the first publication of a short prayer which has become an accepted hymn throughout Christendom, *God be in my head and in my understanding*. An earlier French version appeared in *Horae 1490*. Set to music by Bishop T. B. Strong (1861–1944) and by Sir S. H. Nicholson (1875–1947) amongst others, the setting most used today is without doubt that by Sir Walford Davies (1869–1941). He was Master of the King's Music in 1934, having been organist both of the Temple Church (where Leopold Stokowski, the famous American conductor, was one of his pupils) and at St George's Chapel, Windsor. He was also widely known for his BBC broadcast, *Music and the ordinary listener*.

His setting of *God be in my head* is very moving. I always remember it sung by George Eldridge, the solo tenor in my choir at Brede and Udimore in the 1970s. It is not at all surprising to note that *God be in my head* was said as a prayer before the daily Offices in Henry VIII's time and has also been included in a number of books of private devotions, both then and up to the present day.

> God be in my head, and in my understanding;
> God be in mine eyes, and in my looking;
> God be in my mouth, and in my speaking;
> God be in my heart, and in my thinking;
> God be at mine end, and at my departing.

Good King Wenceslas looked out

'AN ENLIGHTENED AND GOOD MAN'

Of all the carols sung at Christmastide, *Good King Wenceslas* is one of the firm favourites, but few who sing of him so energetically know the story which made the King 'good' and earned him a place among the saints.

We must go back a thousand years to discover this, to the time when the present Czech Republic was the Kingdom of Bohemia, still largely a pagan land where Christianity had, as yet, made little impact.

At the age of 20, the young Wenceslas succeeded his father and, acting on his firmly held Christian principles, immediately made peace with his country's enemies and set about introducing all kinds of reforms. In every city in his realm he built a church, and in his own castle at Prague he established a daily service at which he read the prayers himself. We read that he 'fed and clothed the hungry, protected the widows and children, purchased the release of many hapless prisoners, especially priests, and showed generous hospitality to strangers' (source unknown); he also abolished the gallows and put an end to torture – a remarkable list of achievements for anyone, especially at such a time.

Perhaps not surprisingly he roused considerable opposition from the nobility who found their sources of wealth seriously threatened by the King's reforms, and were no longer able to exploit the peasants as they had done before. Wenceslas' own brother became the leader of the malcontents and plotted his downfall. It was in fact whilst staying at his brother's castle that Wenceslas was set upon and murdered as he entered the church for the early mass. He was only 22, but in his short life as King he had earned his place in legend as an enlightened and good man.

The particular story of the King's act of kindness in trudging through the snow to bring help to a poor man perishing from cold and hunger was created by the carol written by that prolific hymn-writer and translator of the last century, John Mason Neale of East Grinstead in Sussex. *The Oxford Book of Carols* condescendingly describes Neale's *Wenceslas* as 'doggerel' and 'commonplace to the last degree', and hopes that the carol will 'gradually pass into disuse', but one feels that the sure instinct of the British public who hold it in great affection will guarantee its survival for many Christmases to come. Christmas is not real if it is self-centred. The old ideas of 'wealth' and 'rank', as of the 'poor', have changed a great deal, yet the familiar words of the carol strike home to everyone:

> Therefore, Christian men, be sure,
> Wealth or rank possessing,
> He who now will bless the poor,
> Shall himself find blessing.

Wenceslas is commemorated in the official church Calendar on 28 September but the Feast of Stephen falls on Boxing Day, so everyone connects the 'Good King' with 26 December.

Guide me, O thou great Redeemer

'THE "SWEET SINGER" OF PANTYCELYN'

Name a favourite Welsh hymn and almost certainly it will be 'Cwm Rhondda'. Yet it is the name of the tune, not the hymn itself. So let us begin by paying tribute to John Hughes, who composed the rich harmonies that often echo wherever Welsh people gather, be it church or chapel, Albert Hall or football stadium. As a youngster Hughes was doorboy at Glyn Colliery (Llanwit Vardre, Glamorgan), but went on to join the G. W. R. (Great Western Railway) for the rest of his working life. He was a devoted member of Salem Baptist Chapel, where he succeeded his father as Deacon and Precentor (choirmaster) until his death in 1932. 'Cwm Rhondda' was written for a festival at Pontypridd in 1905, as a setting for the already established hymn (see below). What then of the words? The story of their origin concerns a William, a Peter and a John and all of them Williams!

The author William was a widely esteemed poet in his own right, known as the 'Sweet Singer' of Pantycelyn; he died in 1791. He wrote principally in his native Welsh language, and what the Wesleys did for England, William did for Wales. Ordained first into the Anglican ministry, he subsequently became attached to the Calvinistic Methodists and was one of their most gifted preachers. Not many of his hymns survive today, but we still enjoy singing the one for which 'Cwm Rhondda' was written – *Guide me, O thou great Redeemer (Jehovah)*. It is close to Bunyan's theme in *The Pilgrim's Progress*, but this, it seems, is seldom recognized by many who sing the words. It also has a eucharistic note: 'Bread of heaven, feed me now and evermore'.

It was translated into English by Peter Williams of Carmarthen, another Anglican clergyman who joined

51

the Methodists. He published a Welsh Bible in 1767. Then William's son John published a collection of his father's works in 1812. So this great hymn found its way into the English-speaking heritage.

A story is told of a Welshman in Chicago who had 'made good', as they say, and amassed quite a considerable fortune. He made a special point of emphasizing to his Rector that he wanted 'Cwm Rhondda' sung at his funeral when the time came. 'Be sure and see to it,' he said. 'It is very important for a man in my position.' 'It is indeed a fine hymn, but why is it so special for you?' replied the Rector. 'Because it is so definite in the last verse,' came the answer. 'It says: "*Land my safe on Canaan's side*".' The priest concerned told the story to me himself. It actually happened to him with one of his own parishioners. Changing an 'e' to a 'y' made all the difference.

Hail, gladdening Light, of his pure glory poured
O gladsome Light, O Grace

'THE "CANDLELIGHTING HYMN"'

If you were to be asked what is the oldest hymn known to Christians – apart, that is, from the gospel Canticles like the Benedictus and Magnificat (which are of course hymns) and the Sanctus (the 'Holy, Holy, Holy' of the Eucharist) – you would almost certainly have to turn to the famous Greek 'Candlelighting Hymn' of the second century, the best translation of which is still that of John Keble, *Hail, gladdening Light*. It is quoted by St Basil, who died in AD 379, and is said to have been written by a man called Sophronius. By the second century, hymns were regularly sung at both morning and evening worship; for the evening service, being usually at dusk, the title 'Candlelighting Hymn' becomes obviously appropriate.

Hail, gladdening Light, of his pure glory poured
Who is the immortal Father, heavenly, blest,
Holiest of holies, Jesus Christ, our Lord.

Now are we come to the sun's hour of rest,
The lights of evening round us shine,
We hymn the Father, Son, and Holy Spirit divine.

Worthiest art thou at all times to be sung
With undefilèd tongue,
Son of our God, giver of life, alone;
Therefore in all the world thy glories, Lord, they
own.

Without a note of music these words are sheer poetry in themselves and truly inspiring. Small wonder Longfellow included them in his *Golden Legend* translation. Robert

Bridges too made a translation for the *Yattendon Hymnal* of 1899 and his is the version – *O gladsome Light, O grace* – which appears, for example, in *Songs of Praise* and *The English Hymnal*. But, as I have said, Keble's version in *Hymns Ancient and Modern* is undoubtedly the finest. I also prefer Stainer's chant-like setting 'Sebaste', though this is probably more familiar to an older generation of churchgoers then the present one.

For the Festival of Candlemas on 2 February this oldest of Greek hymns seems very appropriate, for Christ as the Light of the World is one of the basic gospel descriptions. There is also the association with the symbolism of the Easter ceremonies and the kindling of the new light of the risen Lord. All in all, the 'Candlelighting Hymn' of so long ago still speaks to us most eloquently of the faith which alone can dispel the gloom and darkness of a troubled world.

Happy are they, they that love God

'THEIR HAPPY BROTHERHOOD'

How true it is! I love this hymn just because it faces up to the facts of life without sentimentalism.

In our hymn books the words are themselves a happy alliance of France and England long before the days of the 'Common Market'. The French connection is centred in eighteenth-century Paris in the person of the Rector of Paris University, Charles Coffin, the greatest Latin scholar France has ever produced. He wrote many famous hymns in Latin and they were published as *Hymni Sacri* in 1736. In various translations they have deservedly found their way into most hymnals and I only have to mention a few for it to be obvious how popular they are – Advent hymns like *On Jordan's bank the Baptist's cry*, Christmas – *God from on high hath heard*, Epiphany – *What star is this that beams so bright*, and other well-established favourites such as *O Holy Spirit, Lord of Grace* and the beautiful evening hymn *As now the sun's declining rays*.

The happy alliance is one of translation, and on the English side leads us to none other than Robert Bridges, the famous Poet Laureate and author of the *Testament of Beauty*. He lived in Yattendon, Berkshire, and from there, with the help of his collaborator H. E. Wooldridge, published in 1899 his *Yattendon Hymnal*. This contained many treasures among them the fine English version of Coffin's *Happy are they*, which the latter had written for Tuesday night Vespers in the Paris Breviary of 1736 (*O quam Juvat*). And another part of the alliance is the superb tune 'Binchester', to which *Happy are they* is always sung. The composer was the great William Croft, who succeeded the even more famous Dr Blow as organist of Westminster Abbey in 1708.

On any reckoning, therefore, both the words and

music are 'classics' and no matter how often they are sung, never seem to lose their appeal. In fact it is, in my view, an ideal choice for a funeral or memorial service, expressing just the right note of what should be in our hearts as we say farewell to a loved one.

> Then shall they know, they that love him
> How all their pain is good
> And death itself cannot unbind
> Their happy brotherhood.

He who would valiant be
(Who would true valour see)

'THE PILGRIM'S PROGRESS HYMN'

It is worthy of note that the two most favoured books throughout Christendom, with the exception of the Bible itself, have been *The Imitation of Christ* by a fifteenth-century German monk and *The Pilgrim's Progress* by an eighteenth-century English prisoner – one a Catholic saint (Thomas à Kempis) and the other a fervent Protestant tinker (John Bunyan). Both men have given us great hymns, loved and cherished by Catholics and Protestants alike the world over. From St Thomas we have *Light's abode, celestial Salem* (see page 76); from John Bunyan we have the universal favourite *Who would true valour see* – the opening line in the author's original – or *He who would valiant be*, in the more modern version by Dr Percy Dearmer.

To find the 'Pilgrim's hymn' we must turn towards the end of Part 2 of *The Pilgrim's Progress*, to the passage where 'Mr Great-heart' and 'Mr Valiant for Truth' are conversing. As Canon Frank Colquhoun points out in his excellent little book, *More Preaching on Favourite Hymns*: 'Before continuing with the story Bunyan pauses and invites the reader to "come hither" and to see in "Valiant" a picture of a brave and faithful pilgrim – "One here will constant be, Come wind, come weather".' Bunyan first published his hymn in 1684 and Dr Percy Dearmer adapted the words for the publication of the *English Hymnal* in 1906. His was indeed a valiant effort and many may prefer the more modern idiom, but to quote another authority on the original version, this time in the American *Hymnal Companion 1940*, Canon Charles Douglas says: 'Bunyan's burly song strikes a new and welcome note in our Hymnal. The quaint sincerity of the words stirs us out of our easy-going dull Christianity to the thrill of great adventure . . . this reminds us of St Paul valiantly battling through manifold disasters in the "care of all the churches".'

The tune sung now almost universally to Bunyan's great hymn is 'Monk's Gate', an English traditional melody adapted by Dr Vaughan Williams.

Holy, holy, holy, Lord God Almighty

'STIRRING WORDS FOR TRINITY SUNDAY'

Tennyson considered it the greatest hymn in the English language. It is certainly one of the most celebrated, having been translated into many different languages in the years since it was written. It first appeared in a magazine called the *Christian Observer* in 1811, over the initials 'D. R.', the final letters of the Christian name and surname of the author Reginald Heber, one of the most illustrious figures in the history of the Anglican Church. Heber wrote *Holy, holy, holy, Lord God Almighty* especially for Trinity Sunday; it was one of a series intended as a hymnal companion to the Book of Common Prayer, illustrating the various seasons of the Christian year. *The Christian Year* was the actual title Heber's contemporary John Keble gave to his own collection of verses published in 1827. Like Keble, Heber was a High Churchman and might have been in sympathy with the outlook of the Tractarians and the Oxford Movement which followed later in the nineteenth century.

After sixteen years as Vicar at Hodnet in Shropshire, Heber, still only 39, was made Bishop of Calcutta – at that time the only Anglican Bishop in the whole of the Eastern hemisphere, with the diocese comprising not only the whole of India and Ceylon but for good measure Australia as well. After only three years of tireless and devoted service, Heber died suddenly in 1826 whilst visiting Trichinopoly in Ceylon for a Confirmation service. He left no less than 57 hymns, several of which are still in use today, such as his lovely vesper *God that madest earth and heaven*, and the famous missionary hymn *From Greenland's icy mountains*.

It is said of Heber that he pioneered a more definite

church hymnody, combining poetic beauty with a more liturgical pattern, which had played little part in the thinking of the hitherto predominantly Evangelical hymn-writers. The trend is clearly evidenced in the hymn which for Tennyson was 'the greatest'. Sung to Dykes' familiar tune 'Nicea', its vigorous language commands genuine poetic dignity whilst being clearly doctrinal in its message for the Feast of the Holy Trinity.

Holy, holy, holy! though the darkness hide thee,
   Though the eye of sinful man thy glory may not see,
Only thou art holy; there is none beside thee,
   Perfect in power, in love, and purity.

How bright these glorious spirits shine
O God, our help in ages past

'THE FATHER OF ENGLISH HYMNODY'

On 25 November at Stoke Newington died the man whom some would describe as the father of all English hymnody, Isaac Watts. It was 1748 and he had been born 74 years earlier, in 1674. His father was a Southampton schoolmaster and a Dissenter (as all Nonconformists were known at that time) and the young Isaac was brought up in a very strict home. There is a delightful story that on one occasion when the family were engaged in morning prayers Isaac was heard to giggle, to the shocked disapproval of his father. On being severely reprimanded and asked to explain his behavour he pointed to a bell rope by the fireplace where he had seen a mouse running up a few minutes before: 'There was a mouse for want of stairs ran up a rope to say his prayers.' His father was not amused and reached for the cane to teach him a lesson, whereupon Isaac immediately continued, 'O father, father, pity take, And I will no more verses make!'

The promise was premature for he went on to make many verses – in fact he wrote over 600 hymns and if we mention but half a dozen of them we see at once that we are listing some great favourites: *Come let us join our cheerful songs, Give me the wings of faith to rise, Before Jehovah's awful throne, Jesus shall reign where'er the sun* and, unquestionably the most famous of them all, *When I survey the wondrous Cross*. Then there is *How bright these glorious spirits shine*, the hymn which Isaac gave us based on the passage in the Book of Revelation which speaks of the redeemed in heaven. It will ring out in a vast number of churches for the All Saints' festival where it conjures up and expresses our faith in the communion of saints, without any suggestion of emotionalism or sentimentalism.

> Midst pastures green he'll lead his flock
> Where living streams appear
> And God the Lord from every eye
> Shall wipe off every tear.

And, of course, there is also the Remembrance-tide hymn O God, *our help in ages past*, based on Psalm 90, sung always to Croft's 'St Anne'. It is strange now to look back and recall that Watts wrote the hymn following the death of Queen Anne and the accession of George I, to mark the end of the persecution of the Dissenters. The references to the 'stormy blast' were directed at the Stuart-supporting Jacobites, at that time very much out of favour, their 'presumptuous boasts and hope blasted'. Yet time puts all such human conflicts behind us and we all look forward to our 'eternal home' where the distinctions of Conformist or Nonconformist, Orthodox or Dissenter will have little place – 'They fly forgotten as a dream/Dies at the opening day'. (See also pages 140–41.)

I cannot tell why he whom angels worship

'BUT THIS I KNOW'

It is pretty safe to say that everyone knows the melody 'The Londonderry Air', whatever our musical taste, for *Danny Boy* is one of those folk songs which have become part and parcel of our national heritage. So when someone had the bright idea of making it the tune for a hymn, it was sure to become widely popular. It was back in 1929 that the then Secretary for the Baptist Missionary Society in London, William Young Fullerton, at the age of 72, produced the hymn beginning *I cannot tell why he whom angels worship*, which, sung to 'The Londonderry Air', has now become familiar to many churches of all denominations. Fullerton was not Irish himself but he published his hymn strong in the faith that Christ's kingdom must be for everyone – all people, in all lands – and that whatever doubts we may have are more than compensated for by the certainties of the Christian gospel. ('I cannot tell' is dispelled by the the opening words of the second part of each verse of the hymn, 'But this I know'.) The words are not included in a number of hymnals so I give them in full so that you may judge for yourself:

I cannot tell why he whom angels worship,
Should set his love upon the sons of men,
Or why, as Shepherd, he should seek the wanderers,
To bring them back, they know not how or when.
But this I know, that he was born of Mary
When Bethlem's manger was his only home,
And that he lived at Nazareth and laboured,
And so the Saviour, Saviour of the world, is come.

I cannot tell how silently he suffered,
As with his peace he graced this place of tears,

Or how his heart upon the cross was broken,
The crown of pain to three-and-thirty years.
But this I know, he heals the broken-hearted,
And stays our sin and calms our lurking fear,
And lifts the burden from the heavy-laden,
For yet the Saviour, Saviour of the world is here.

I cannot tell how he will win the nations,
How he will claim his earthly heritage,
How satisfy the needs and aspirations
Of east and west, of sinner and of sage.
But this I know, all flesh shall see his glory,
And he shall reap the harvest he has sown,
And some glad day his sun shall shine in splendour,
When he the Saviour, Saviour of the world is known.

I cannot tell how all the lands shall worship,
When at his bidding every storm is stilled,
Or who can say how great the jubilation,
When all the hearts of men with love are filled.
But this I know, the skies will thrill with rapture,
And myriad, myriad human voices sing,
And earth to heav'n, and heav'n to earth, will
    answer:
'At last the Saviour, Saviour of the world, is King!'

William Fullerton died in 1932 at the age of 75. He had the satisfaction of knowing by then that he had left behind him a hymn which multitudes love to sing.

Immortal, invisible, God only wise

'SCOT'S WORDS WITH FINE WELSH TUNE'

It is often difficult to determine whether a hymn's words or the tune to which they are most often sung constitutes the popularity which the hymn enjoys. This is certainly true of Walter Chalmers Smith's *Immortal, invisible, God only wise*. The tune which is used most widely is the fine old Welsh one 'St Denio' and has all the virtues of simplicity, melody and fine harmony to commend it – and for good congregational singing no very high notes! There is little more to say about it other than that it is based on a Welsh folk song, *Can Mlynedd i'nawr*, and first appeared as a hymn tune in 1839.

But the words too are very fine in their own right and are also nineteenth century, though not from Wales but from Scotland, for Walter Chalmers Smith was born in Aberdeen in 1824 and became in 1893 Moderator of the Free Church of Scotland after a ministry in Islington, Glasgow and Edinburgh. He died at Kinbuck in Perthshire in 1918, on 20 September, at the good old age of 84. *Immortal, invisible* was published in 1867 in *Hymns of the Christian Life*; well over a century later it seems to be the only one of the collection that has effectively survived.

Cardinal Newman's *Lead kindly light* (see pages 99–101) was chosen as the only hymn that could satisfy the 'Parliament of Religions' held in the 1880s in Chicago, USA, and so earned for itself the title the 'Ecumenical hymn'. But I suspect *Immortal invisible* would run it a very close rival. There is nothing in the words of this hymn which could not be sung with equal sincerity by Jew, Christian and Muslim. Not even the name of Christ is mentioned and there is no doxology. The 'doctrine' it enshrines is the universal one of God the Father and Creator of all being. Yet precisely because this is part and parcel of basic Christian belief it is not surprising that the hymn is to be found in almost every Christian hymnal.

Unresting, unhasting, and silent as light,
Nor wanting, nor wasting, thou rulest in might;
Thy justice like mountains high soaring above
Thy clouds which are fountains of goodness and love.

Newman in his *Dream of Gerontius* speaks of the vision of the Godhead and then wants to hide his face from the dazzling light. Smith expresses the same sentiments eloquently:

Great Father of glory, pure Father of light,
Thine angels adore thee, all veiling their sight;
All laud we would render; O help us to see
'Tis only the splendour of light hideth thee.

Jesu, lover of my soul

'THE SENTRY WHO WOULD NOT SHOOT'

Charles Wesley, who died in 1788, must have the distinction of being the most prolific hymn-writer of all time. In more than 50 volumes the total reaches a staggering figure of more than 7,000! Not surprisingly, perhaps, with such an achievement he can also lay claim to being the author of not a few almost universal favourites. Wesley wrote, of course, in the first place for the 'people called Methodists', and with his brother John was one of the leading personalities in the movement that was later to become the Methodist Church.

But, of all these Methodist hymns that have now become the common inheritance of all Churches, there is one which would almost certainly claim the accolade as the most popular and best loved of them all – its first words are: 'Jesu, lover of my soul'. Various stories have been told about how Wesley came to write this famous hymn. One tells us that during a storm on an Atlantic crossing (he went to America with brother John in 1735) a seabird took refuge in his lap. Another has it that he wrote the verses while sheltering under a hedge in Ireland, hiding from a band of ruffians that were pursuing him. But there is one true story about the hymn which is certainly worth repeating. During the American Civil War a Confederate sentry heard singing coming from the enemy lines and tracking down the singer, was about to shoot him down, when he heard the words 'Cover my defenceless head, With the shadow of thy wing'. Overcome as a fellow Christian believer, he lowered his rifle and the singer lived to become an evangelist preacher after the war.

One day, on a steamer on the Potomac River, the same 'Yankee' soldier-turned-preacher was singing the same words again. One of his fellow passengers who heard him was none other than the Confederate sentry who years before had spared his life. We can imagine the mutual joy of the two men when they at last met again in this strange way.

The American writer Henry Ward Beecher declared, 'I would rather have written *Jesu, lover of my soul* than have the fame of all the kings that ever lived upon earth.' Many would agree with him for there can be no question other than that this hymn is indeed a masterpiece and, deservedly, a very great favourite. Many, particularly of the older generation, still love to sing it to Dykes' 'Hollingside' but the tune which really seems to catch the whole spirit of the words and inspire real emotion is Joseph Parry's fine 'Aberystwyth' – but then the Welsh are almost as good at hymn tunes as Charles Wesley at hymns!

(See also *Love divine, all loves excelling* and *O thou who camest from above* on pages 82–83).

Just as I am, without one plea

'THE INVALID'S HYMN FROM BRIGHTON'

Charlotte Elliott was only 32 when she was smitten by a disease which was to keep her confined to a wheelchair for the rest of her long life (incredibly she lived to the ripe old age of 82). Her brother was a vicar in Brighton, and their father a member of the famous 'Clapham Sect', a group of Evangelicals closely associated with the foundation of The British and Foreign Bible Society in 1804.

In 1831 (Charlotte was 45 by then), her brother was arranging a bazaar to raise funds for St Mary's Hall, a school for poor clergy daughters. Charlotte felt completely useless watching everyone else busily preparing for the bazaar. Earnestly she prayed for divine guidance. Her prayer was answered and she was inspired to do what she could do best. Taking up pen and paper, she wrote the verses which since that time have brought faith and inspiration to many thousands. Inspired by John 6.37 – 'Him that cometh unto me I will in no wise cast out' – she wrote her hymn which began:

> Just as I am, without one plea
> But that thy blood was shed for me,
> And that thou bidd'st me come to thee,
>   O Lamb of God, I come.

Published in leaflet form in 1835, the hymn caught on at once and was even read by the poet Wordsworth to his sister Dora as she lay dying. In later years Charlotte's brother is recorded as saying that her hymn had done much more for preaching the gospel than all his sermons put together! Charlotte also wrote several other popular hymns, among them *Christian, seek not yet repose*, much loved by a previous generation. She died in 1871, 'A lover of nature, a lover of souls and a true lover of Christ'.

Hymn-writing was probably in the family genes, because Charlotte's niece Emily Elliott also left us a really great hymn in 1873, *Thou didst leave thy throne and thy Kingly crown*. Timothy Matthews' fine tune 'Margaret' fits Emily's words splendidly and is justly popular.

Two tunes are still in general use for *Just as I am*: one (much loved by the older generation) is Henry Smart's 'Misericordia', and the other is 'Saffron Walden' by Arthur Brown.

Lead us, heavenly Father, lead us

'PROVIDED, PARDONED, GUIDED'

There must be few who do not know and value *Lead us, heavenly Father, lead us*, a hymn widely used at weddings and funerals as well as in what we might call the more normal Sunday repertoire. Yet I doubt whether most of us will even have heard of the author before. His name was James Edmeston and he died in 1867 at Homerton in East London where he was Churchwarden.

James Edmeston was a practising architect and surveyor until his death and it would be interesting to know if there are any others in his profession who could boast of having written over 2,000 hymns! He wrote a new one each week for his family Sunday morning devotions, though *Lead us, heavenly Father, lead us* is really the only one that has lasted and found its way into pretty well every hymnal published. Not surprisingly, I feel, for this hymn has an obvious simplicity and directness without any of the rather sloppy sentimentality that often characterizes Victorian worship.

> Guard us, guide us, keep us, feed us,
>   For we have no help but thee;
> Yet possessing every blessing
>   If our God our Father be.

Just about everybody sings *Lead us, heavenly Father, lead us* to 'Mannheim' which is from a chorale by the German (Berlin) composer Friedrich Filitz who died in 1876. He has given us two other very well-known tunes as well: 'Caswall', for the Passiontide hymn *Glory be to Jesus*, and 'Capetown' for the Trinitytide hymn *Three in One, and One in Three*.

The latter brings us back full circle to Mr Edmeston

and *Lead us, heavenly Father, lead us*, for this hymn is
entirely trinitarian, each verse being a prayer to 'Father',
'Saviour' and 'Spirit of our God, descending', so that
'Thus provided, pardoned, guided/Nothing can our peace
destroy'.

Let all mortal flesh keep silence
Lord Jesus Christ, you have come to us

'EUCHARISTIC HYMNS,
ANCIENT AND MODERN'

Amongst the Top Twenty in my Poll were several eucharistic hymns, two of them popular today. One dates back right to the earliest times, and comes from the ancient Liturgy of St James of Jerusalem (in the late fourth or early fifth century); the other is the fine hymn very much from our own time, Canon Patrick Appleford's *Lord Jesus Christ, you have come to us* – ancient and modern with a vengeance!

Let all mortal flesh keep silence – the Cherubic Hymn in the Greek Orthodox Eucharist – is sung as the sacred elements are brought to the Sanctuary in procession, so beginning the Liturgy of the Faithful. We are indebted for the fine English translation from the Greek to a great Victorian Classical scholar, Gerard Moultrie (1829–85), son of a Rector of Rugby, who became Warden of St James College, South Leigh. He had a great command of language and rather modestly signed his many translations and other writings 'DP' ('Desiderius Pastor' or 'Beloved Pastor'). The words of the hymn in question breathe the very spirit of worship:

> Let all mortal flesh keep silence,
>   And with fear and trembling stand;
> Ponder nothing earthly-minded,
>   For with blessing in his hand
> Christ our God to earth descendeth,
>   Our full homage to demand.

A saintly old lady whom I buried not so long ago (having reached the age of 106!) told me of the many changes she had experienced during her long life – some for the better and some for the worse. One thing which she found very distressing was the lack of what she called 'Divine Silence' in so much of today's worship. 'I was brought up to "keep silence" in church, as the old hymn puts it,' she said, 'but now it's anything but – everyone chatters before the service begins and children run about all over the place, even during the Eucharist.' I think she had a point.

The majestic tune which has become almost inseparable from Moultrie's words is a seventeenth-century French carol from Picardy (*Jésus Christ s'habille en pauvre*) found in Tiersot's *Melodies* in Paris (1887).

Patrick Appleford was born in 1924 and *Lord Jesus Christ, you have come to us* is one of his best hymns. He wrote the words and composed the tune, which has the same name as the hymn, and they go together admirably. It is safe to predict that the hymn will certainly last and be ranked as among the finest in our twentieth-century hymnody. Appleford was a Canon Residentiary of Chelmsford Cathedral from 1978 to 1990, which meant that he was one of the people responsible for the maintenance of the cathedral and its services.

> Lord Jesus Christ,
> You have come to us,
> You are one with us,
>   Mary's Son;
> Cleansing our souls from all their sin,
> Pouring your love and goodness in;
> Jesus, our love for you we sing,
>   Living Lord.
>
> Lord Jesus Christ,
> Now and every day
> Teach us how to pray,
>   Son of God.
> You have commanded us to do
> This in remembrance, Lord of you:

Into our lives your power breaks through,
    Living Lord.

Lord Jesus Christ,
I would come to you,
Live my life for you,
    Son of God.
All your commands I know are true,
Your many gifts will make me new,
Into my life your power breaks through,
    Living Lord.

'NOW WITH GLADNESS,
NOW WITH COURAGE'

This hymn was written by Thomas Haemerken of Kempen, near Dusseldorf, Germany. He is known historically as St Thomas à Kempis and his bestselling book is *The Imitation of Christ*, which, ever since it was written in the fourteenth century, has sold more copies in every language than any other publication except the Bible. Born in 1379, our author lived to the great age of 91 – quite exceptional in those days – and died in 1471.

He also wrote a number of spiritual songs and one of these has been popularized in the English translation of the great hymnographer John Mason Neale of East Grinstead. Thomas called it *Jerusalem Luminosa* but Neale shortened Jerusalem to Salem, and so that lovely hymn now begins: 'Light's abode, celestial Salem/Vision whence true peace doth spring'. The fourth verse in particular is a wonderful affirmation of Christian faith and our glorious Eastertide hope, and so is also most appropriate for singing at funerals.

> O how glorious and resplendent,
> Fragile body, shalt thou be,
> When imbued with so much beauty,
> Full of health, and strong, and free,
> Full of vigour, full of pleasure
> That shall last eternally.

The tune usually sung to *Light's abode* is the well-known 'Regent's Square', composed in 1866 by Henry Thomas Smart who was a very gifted musician and built the organs at the Town Halls in both Glasgow and Leeds.

Now with gladness, now with courage,
   Bear the burden on thee laid,
That hereafter these thy labours
   May with endless gifts be paid,
And in everlasting glory
   Thou with brightness be arrayed.

Lord, enthroned in heavenly splendour

'RISEN, ASCENDED, GLORIFIED'

There are few churches nowadays where periodically Prebendary George Hugh Bourne's majestic verses are not sung at the Sunday morning Eucharist – whatever the church tradition of a particular parish. This is the more true because of Sir George Martin's great tune 'St Helen' which he composed specially for the hymn in the 1889 edition of *Hymns Ancient and Modern*. It is a lively, buoyant tune, set at a pitch which lends itself to good congregational singing!

Originally the hymn had no less than ten verses, although only five are used in most of the more modern hymnals, and was just one of seven post-Communion hymns especially written for the boys of St Edmund's School, Salisbury. Bourne was headmaster there for some eleven years in the latter part of the nineteenth century. Ordained in 1864, he devoted his life to educational purposes and was also Sub-Dean of the Cathedral at Salisbury for fourteen years.

Lord, enthroned in heavenly splendour was first written for the Ascension Day festival but it is suitable really for any time throughout the year.

> Lord, enthroned in heavenly splendour
> First-begotten from the dead,
> Thou alone, our strong defender,
> Liftest up thy people's head.
> Alleluia!
> Jesu, true and living Bread.
>
> Here our humblest homage pay we;
> Here in loving reverence bow;
> Here for faith's discernment pray we,
> Lest we fail to know thee now.

Alleluia!
Thou art here, we ask not how.

The hymn also speaks of 'heavenly Manna' and of the time when Moses found water in the desert ('Stricken Rock with streaming side'), so, essentially, it is scriptural in its imagery, depicting both the incarnation and the sacrifice of Calvary, as well as the victorious Easter and Ascension themes:

> Paschal Lamb, thine offering, finished
> Once for all when thou wast slain,
> In its fullness undiminished
> Shall for evermore remain,
> Alleluia!
> Cleansing souls from every stain.
>
> Life-imparting heavenly Manna,
> Stricken Rock with streaming side,
> Heaven and earth with loud hosanna
> Worship thee, the Lamb who died,
> Alleluia!
> Risen, ascended, glorified.

Lord of all hopefulness, Lord of all joy

'THE "MRS MINIVER HYMN" FROM RYE'

In my twenties, I regarded *Mrs Miniver* as one of the best movies I had ever seen and I expect there are many others who will remember this wartime film with as much affection as I do. The film tells the story of the lady of the manor (Mrs Miniver) whose only son is killed as a pilot in the Battle of Britain. The parish church is destroyed in an air raid and the whole village is involved. What I did not know then was that the author of the best-selling novel (on which the film was based) would also be the author of one of my best-loved modern hymns. It was called the 'All-day hymn' and was often sung at school assembly and the like. Now I am glad to say it has found its way into general use in churches of all demoninations everywhere: *Lord of all hopefulness, Lord of all joy.*

The author used the pen-name Jan Struther – her family name was Anstruther and she was born in London and then went to live at Playden, near Rye. At one time she was on the Editorial Board of *The Times*. A great friend of Dr Percy Dearmer, responsible for the creation of the hymnal *Songs of Praise* (1931), she composed this lovely hymn deliberately at his request to fit the old Irish folk tune 'Slane', to which it is sung universally. She married a Polish airman and became Mrs Joyce Placzek.

Another of her hymns, *When Mary brought her treasure*, is a very lovely one for Candlemas Day, and, very appropriately, is still sung every year at the Rye Deanery Candlemas Service.

> No eye of man could measure,
> The joy upon her face.
> He was but six weeks old,
> Her plaything and her pleasure,
> Her silver and her gold.

When the child grew to become the carpenter of Nazareth, our author again has just the right words:

> Lord of all eagerness, Lord of all faith,
> Whose strong hands were skilled at the plane and the
> lathe,
> Be there at our labours, and give us, we pray,
> Your strength in our hearts, Lord, at the noon of the
> day.

And Jan Struther needed all the strength she could get, for cancer struck her down in early middle age. Indeed, she was only 52 when she died in America in 1953. In the light of this, the closing lines of her 'All-day hymn' take on an added poignancy:

> Lord of all gentleness, Lord of all calm,
> Whose voice is contentment, whose presence is balm,
> Be there at our sleeping, and give us, we pray,
> Your peace in our hearts, Lord, at the end of the day.

Love divine, all loves excelling
O thou who camest from above

'JOY OF HEAVEN TO EARTH COME DOWN'

Suppose you opened your hymn book and found that suddenly a long list of your – and everyone else's – favourites had suddenly vanished: no *Hark, the herald-angels sing*, or *Lo, he comes with clouds descending*, no *Soldiers of Christ, arise*, or *Christ, whose glory fills the skies*, no *Let saints on earth in concert sing*, and no *Jesu, lover of my soul* or *Love divine, all loves excelling* – the hymn which came fifth in my Poll.

We cannot begin to express our gratitude to the hymn-writer who left us with so many real favourites: Charles Wesley, who died on 29 March 1788. Incredible though it sounds, he wrote over 6,000 hymns all told and it is safe to predict that many of them will still be sung a century hence. *Love divine* is a favourite hymn for weddings everywhere. Charles got the idea from a popular song of the time, from the poet Dryden's play *King Arthur*: *Fairest isle, all isles excelling*, set to the music of the great English composer Henry Purcell. The hymn is really a prayer addressed to Christ, that his love should come to each of us and find in our hearts a 'humble dwelling':

> Finish then thy new creation,
>   Pure and spotless let us be;
> Let us see thy great salvation,
>   Perfectly restored in thee,
> Changed from glory into glory,
>   Till in heaven we take our place,
> Till we cast our crowns before thee,
>   Lost in wonder, love, and praise.

Strangely enough, Charles first wrote 'sinless' rather than 'spotless' and it was his famous brother John who asked him to make the alteration, based on 2 Corinthians 5.17 where Paul speaks of Christ's 'new creation', an idea carried further in the lovely phrase 'changed from glory into glory' (2 Corinthians again). The truly sanctified will be enabled to live strong and holy lives.

John Stainer's tune 'Love Divine' first appeared in the 1889 edition of *Hymns Ancient and Modern* and is still much loved by many. The Welsh tune 'Blaenwern' is now also increasingly popular, composed by William Penfro Rowlands (1860–1937). Purcell's melody is still used in some Methodist circles, whilst others sing the hymn to another fine Welsh tune, 'Hyfrydol', by R. H. Pritchard, familiar as the now universally popular tune for *Alleluia sing to Jesus!*.

Another great hymn by Charles Wesley – one that proved to be very popular with the clergy in my Poll – is:

> O thou who camest from above
>   The pure celestial fire to impart,
> Kindle a flame of sacred love
>   On the mean altar of my heart.
>
> There let it for thy glory burn
>   With inextinguishable blaze,
> And trembling to its source return
>   In humble prayer and fervent praise.

This appeared in his *Scripture Hymns* in 1762 (two verses of eight lines each). It is usually sung to his grandson's (Samuel Sebastian Wesley) tune 'Hereford', published in *The European Psalmist* (1872).

John was the fifteenth child, and Charles the eighteenth child, of an eighteenth-century parson, the Rector of Epworth in Lincolnshire – such a large-sized family makes the modern mind boggle! Both brothers were considered 'High Church' for their day and wanted much more discipline and method in their spiritual and religious practice, saying Matins and Evensong daily and receiving more frequent Communion. They formed a 'holy club' and were nicknamed 'Methodists'. All who became Methodists were still encouraged to frequent their parish church for the sacraments, whilst having their separate meetings for other worship and study of the Scriptures. Both brothers remained Anglicans and Charles, when he came to die, asked specifically that he be buried in his parish churchyard of Marylebone. It was only later, with both Charles and John dead, that their followers separated from the Established Church. It is easy for us with the benefit of hindsight to see the folly and mistakes of both sides in the split, but it is well to remember that as recently as the 1970s it did not prove possible to end the schism, as many of us had hoped.

My song is love unknown
Jerusalem on high

'MY FRIEND INDEED'

It is hard for us to imagine the trauma and heartache of our forefathers when they experienced the terrible Civil War 350 or so years ago. Charles I was beheaded and became King Charles the Martyr (with several churches in the UK dedicated in his name). The only military dictatorship we have ever known followed when the Book of Common Prayer was banished and observance of Christmas forbidden. There was general rejoicing at the Restoration under Charles II, and then trauma again under James II. It was from this troubled period of English history that Samuel Crossman, Dean of Bristol, gave us two great hymns, *Jerusalem on high* and *My song is love unknown*.

The first, sung to the tune 'Christchurch', appears in most hymnals:

> My song and city is
> My home whene'er I die
> The centre of my bliss
> O happy place! when I shall be
> My God, with thee, to see thy face.

For some reason, *My song is love unknown* seems to have been overlooked until recent times but now appears in every reputable hymnal and has become widely popular, thanks not a little to the fine tune 'Love unknown' which John Ireland provided, at the request of Geoffrey Shaw (whose setting of the Eucharist to folk mass tunes is very popular). Ireland is said to have composed it on a scrap of paper in just fifteen minutes! Dean Crossman's verses are very fine, emotional without being sentimental, and provide us with one of our very best Passiontide hymns, singing the thanks and praise of the Church for all that was done on Calvary and in the glorious resurrection.

Here might I stay and sing,
  No story so divine;
Never was love, dear King,
  Never was grief like thine!
This is my friend,
  In whose sweet praise
  I all my days
  Could gladly spend.

Now thank we all our God

'NUN DANKET'

'Nun danket alle Gott' (*Now thank we all our God*) is known as the German Te Deum and it is such a fine hymn that it has been translated into many other languages, of which Catherine Winkworth's English version is a notable one. Whenever it is sung to Crüger's majestic tune it stirs the heart as it has stirred the hearts of thousands, indeed millions, since it was first used more than three centuries ago at Eilenburg in Saxony.

It was written at the time of the 'Thirty Years' War' (1618–1648), during which the little town had suffered grievously and been sacked by both Austrians and Swedes. Because Eilenburg was a walled city, refugees from miles around had poured in, thinking they would find safety, and with such overcrowding the carnage was appalling when plague struck the district and killed over 8,000. The only clergyman there was the Lutheran Archdeacon Martin Rinkart and he was obliged to take as many as 50 funerals a day, including that of his own wife! Famine followed the plague and caused still more deaths. We can imagine the relief and joy which must have greeted the news of the signing of the Peace of Westphalia in 1648. The Elector (or Prince) of Saxony ordered thanksgiving services to be held in every church and even himself selected the text for the sermons – from Ecclesiasticus 50.22–3: 'Now bless ye the God of all, Who everywhere doeth great things, Who exalteth our days from the womb and dealeth with us according to His mercy. May He grant us joyful hearts and may peace be in our days for ever.'

Perhaps, as Martin Rinkart pondered on this text, he found himself forming the words which were to make his famous hymn and which were used then at his own

Eilenburg thanksgiving. It has been said that 'no words can ever voice more perfectly the gratitude of the human heart' (source unknown) and I think few would disagree. The hymn faithfully echoes the Elector's apocryphal text:

Now thank we all our God,
With heart and hands and voices,
Who wondrous things hath done,
In whom his world rejoices;
Who from our mother's arms
Hath blessed us on our way
With countless gifts of love,
And still is ours today.

Johann Crüger's fine tune 'Nun danket' has had several variations since it first appeared in *Praxis Pietatis Melica*, a famous collection of hymn tunes published by Crüger in 1647, which was very popular and went through numerous editions. The version used in most hymnals is from Mendelssohn's *Hymn of Praise* (1840).

O come, o come, Emmanuel

'SINGING FOR THEIR SUPPER'

> To provide a fire continually in the common hall for
> the monks to warm themselves and to have always a
> hogshead of wine for the keeping of Advent's Great
> O's together with provision of figs and walnuts.

According to the *Rites of Durham* this was one of the
duties of the Commoners' Checker (a monastic steward)
and behind it lies the story of one of our best-loved
Advent hymns. Traditionally, the antiphon before the
Magnificat at Vespers on the days leading up to Christmas consisted of a series of verses expressing joy at the
coming of Christ as Saviour and using the various
scriptural titles ascribed to the Messiah. Introduced into
the liturgy before the ninth century, they welcome Jesus
as 'O Wisdom', 'O Lord of Hosts', 'O Root of Jesse', 'O
Key of David', 'O Dayspring from on high', 'O King of the
nations', 'O Emmanuel', and finally, on 23 December, 'O
Virgin of virgins'.

The plainsong chant to which these anthems were
sung made great play on the 'O' of each one, with many
notes rising and falling, so that they became known as the
'Great O's of Advent' and often specific antiphons were
assigned to particular monks. The Abbot sang 'O
Wisdom', the Prior 'O Lord of Hosts', the Cellarer 'O Key
of David' and so on. Each monastic officer on the day he
sang his 'Great O' was also expected to provide suitable
hospitality for everyone afterwards – 'singing for their
supper', which may well be the origin of this old saying.

The Book of Common Prayer clearly implies that these
Advent anthems were sung long after the Dissolution of
the Monasteries. Indeed they still are used today in many
of our cathedrals. The 1662 Prayer Book Calendar for

December has 16 December marked as 'O *Sapientia*' (Wisdom), though the others are not specified as such. Then in 1710 an anonymous compiler in Cologne had the idea of putting all the O's together as a hymn and singing them to the Kyrie melody from an old French missal. In 1851 this hymn was translated into English by that most noted of all our hymn translators, John Mason Neale of East Grinstead, who contributed one-eighth of all the hymns published in the First Edition of *Hymns Ancient and Modern*.

So it was that the Advent Hymn *O come, O come, Emmanuel* was born and is now included in almost every hymnal in the Christian world. As we sing, it is not difficult to imagine the old monks intoning their 'Great O's' in the candlelight of their choir stalls. Whether we shall have some wine, figs and walnuts round our fire when we get home from church is up to us! But what a fascinating story it is and how it still inspires us to greet the coming of our infant Redeemer:

> Rejoice, rejoice! Emmanuel
> Shall come to thee, O Israel.

O Jesus, I have promised

'TO THE END OF THE ROAD'

Sir Harry Lauder's famous song from the early 1900s, *Keep right on to the end of the road*, is still popular with older people today though I doubt if many of the younger generation have even heard of Sir Harry, let alone his songs! Thankfully, however, many of them have heard, and indeed frequently still sing, a hymn on the same theme – *O Jesus, I have promised* – a firm favourite of young and old alike. The hymn-writer's name was John Ernest Bode, son of William Bode, at that time (1816) head of the Foreign Department of the General Post Office. John grew up to be a notable scholar, and when Matthew Arnold was elected Professor of Poetry at Oxford in 1855 John Bode was only one vote behind him. As far as hymns go, however, only his fine *O Jesus, I have promised* has survived.

How it came to be written at all is very interesting. John had been ordained in 1841 and was Rector of Castle Camps in Cambridgeshire. His two sons and one daughter were all presented for Confirmation together in 1866 and John decided the occasion merited a special hymn, and so he wrote one! It was published first as a leaflet by SPCK in 1868 and soon became popular everywhere, not only for Confirmations but as a general hymn of Christian discipleship. It is certainly very evocative as such:

> O let me see thy footmarks,
>   And in them plant mine own;
> My hope to follow duly
>   Is in thy strength alone;
> O guide me, call me, draw me,
>   Uphold me to the end;

And then in heaven receive me,
My Saviour and my Friend.

One of Bode's stanzas is now omitted and one wonders why? Judge for yourself:

O let me see thy features,
The look that once could make
So many a true disciple
Leave all things for thy sake;
The look that beamed on Peter
When he thy name denied,
The look that draws thy loved ones
Close to thy pierced side.

The Harry Lauder generation always sang John Bode's verses to a tune called 'Day of rest' but nowadays there are several others, notably 'Thornbury', composed by Basil Harwood for that other fine hymn *Thy hand, O God, has guided* (see page 131). There is also 'Wolvercote', specially written for the boys of Lancing College by W. H. Ferguson. But whatever the tune, the words are imperative – we must keep right on to the end – for that is our promise at Baptism and Confirmation and throughout our life.

O Lord my God, when I in awesome wonder

'HOW GREAT THOU ART'

One of the hymns that was completely unknown when I was a choirboy at All Saints, Penarth, in the 1920s, has rocketed to fame in recent decades and is now numbered among most people's favourites: *How great thou art*. It is commonly attributed to Russian origins with the author unknown. Yet it really comes not from Russia at all, but from Sweden, for it was there, at Monsteras in southern Sweden, some two hundred miles south of Stockholm, that it was written by Pastor Carl Boberg in the summer of 1885. Cecil Kerr, writing in the *Church of Ireland Gazette*, told the true story as it was related to him by Ralph Floden, an organist in Sweden who was visiting the Christian Renewal Centre in Ireland. His father, Alfred Floden, had been a great friend of Carl Boberg and so had passed on the story at first hand to his son.

Ralph Floden told how Boberg was converted to Christianity after his previous time at sea (like another famous hymnographer, John Newton, who gave us *Glorious things of thee are spoken* and *How sweet the name of Jesus sounds*, amongst many others). In 1885 Boberg was caught in a fierce thunderstorm at Monsteras and eventually finding shelter, as he looked out of the window, saw a giant rainbow stretching over the whole Gulf of Monsteras (part of the Baltic Sea). At the same time the bells of the local church began to peal and combined to inspire him to write the verses which have since gone round the world. Originally in nine verses, the hymn was published in 1886. Some time later a Swedish missionary, duly impressed by Boberg's verses, translated them into Russian and so in 1949 they were 'discovered' by Stuart Hine, who translated them in turn into English. Dr Billy Graham came upon this translation in the USA and was so taken by the words that he decided to use them in his 1955 Crusade in Toronto. In 1957 in New York it was sung 99 times. The rest is history.

So a great hymn eventually reached us. *How great thou art* has already earned its rightful place among the fine hymns of Christendom, and I have no doubt will still be sung a century and more hence.

The tune to which this great hymn is sung is the Swedish folk melody to which Boberg's verses were set in 1891.

> O Lord my God! When I in awesome wonder
> Consider all the works thy hand hath made,
> I see the stars, I hear the mighty thunder,
> Thy power throughout the universe displayed;
>
> Then sings my soul, my Saviour God, to thee,
> How great thou art! How great thou art!
>
> And when I think that God his Son not sparing,
> Sent him to die – I scarce can take it in.
> That on the cross my burden gladly bearing,
> He bled and died to take away my sin:
>
> When Christ shall come with shout of acclamation
> And take me home – what joy shall fill my heart!
> Then shall I bow in humble adoration
> And there proclaim, my God, How great thou art!

O Love that will not let me go

'THE BROKEN ENGAGEMENT'

> I regard this as one of the most moving and profound hymns in the English Language. It is one of very few hymns which tackle that most difficult area of human experience for the Christian believer, the reality of suffering, and which does so not in a sentimental or cloying way but in a spirit of Christian hope and with an intense sense of the mystery of life.

So says Dr Ian Bradley in *The Penguin Book of Hymns* – and rightly so. Some hymns have a particular story connected with the person who wrote them. This is certainly true of George Matheson's famous hymn *O Love that wilt not let me go*. Matheson was engaged to be married but by a great misfortune he became blind. His fiancée on hearing of his blindness wrote to him breaking off their engagement. Perhaps the memory of that pain was the inspiration for the verses he later composed:

> O Love that will not let me go,
> I rest my weary soul in Thee:
> I give Thee back the life I owe,
> That in Thine ocean depths its flow,
> May richer, fuller be.

> O Joy that seekest me through pain,
> I cannot close my heart to Thee:
> I trace the rainbow through the rain,
> And feel the promise is not vain
> That morn shall tearless be.

'The rainbow through the rain' – how often others have found comfort, as Matheson himself did, when tragedy or bereavement comes to them. He was Minister of the parish of Innellan, Argyllshire, and afterwards wrote of his famous hymn:

It was composed with extreme rapidity and it seemed to me its construction only occupied a few minutes. I felt myself more in the position of one who was being dictated to than of an original artist. I was suffering from great mental distress and the hymn was the fruit of my pain.

It is only fair to add that the story of the hymn following the broken engagement is disputed and that another version of Matheson's motives in writing this hymn is entirely different. At a time of great confusion in people's minds between 'science' and 'religion', Matheson himself had grave doubts but that the Divine Love would not let him go. With sudden realization of this tremendous fact he sat down and quickly penned his verses.

Whichever way it was, we still have a magnificent hymn which has inspired, and still inspires, Christians of widely different traditions. It is usually sung to the tune 'St Margaret', written for it by Dr Albert Peace, Organist of Glasgow Cathedral. For him, too, it was a rapid composition, completed while on holiday in the Isle of Arran: 'I may say that the ink of the first note was hardly dry when I had finished the tune.'

It is worth noting that Matheson himself said that in the famous couplet, 'From the ground there blossoms red life that shall endless be', he was using red as the symbolic colour of that sacrificial life which blooms only by giving of itself:

> I lay in dust life's glory dead,
> And from the ground there blossoms red,
> Life that shall endless be.

'ONWARD, CHRISTIAN SOLDIERS'

Marching hymns and marching tunes have often been amongst the most popular with young and old alike and surely one of the most popular of all is Sabine Baring-Gould's *Onward, Christian soldiers*. Its rousing tune, 'St Gertrude', was composed by Sir Arthur Sullivan, of Gilbert and Sullivan fame, who is reputed to have been paid only a couple of guineas for composing it.

It was over a century ago, in 1864, that the new curate at Horbury Bridge in Yorkshire decided to write a new hymn for the 'Whit Walk', or procession of the Sunday School children, a really great event in the North then, if not so much now. Baring-Gould sat up half the night to finish his verses and the next day *Onward, Christian soldiers* was heard for the first time. It was an instant favourite and we can well imagine the youngsters singing out: 'We are not divided/All one body we' – true of their Sunday School if not of the Church at large. In fact, Baring-Gould did subsequently make an amended version which appears in some hymnals: 'Though divisions harass/All one body we'.

Some modern hymnals omit *Onward, Christian soldiers* completely as being too militaristic and triumphalistic, but this is to miss the whole point. All of us should ponder Baring-Gould's stirring words of real faith:

> Gates of Hell can never
>   'Gainst that Church prevail;
> We have Christ's own promise,
>   And that cannot fail!

Later on, Baring-Gould gave us another finé marching hymn by translating the work of Bernhardt Ingemann,

Professor of Zealand University, Denmark: *Through the night of doubt and sorrow*. This is usually sung nowadays to Martin Shaw's inspiring tune 'Marching' or to 'St Oswald' by John Bacchus Dykes. Professor Ingemann took the theme of pilgrimage, the Old Testament story of the Israelites journeying to the promised land, guided by the pillar of fire by night and the cloud by day. This he applied to the Christian Church on earth journeying to Paradise – as the Book of Common Prayer Collect puts it, passing 'through things temporal that we finally lose not the things eternal'. Baring-Gould's English translation succeeds in conveying the strength and beauty of the Danish writer's words as a great song of hope.

> One the object of our journey,
>   One the faith which never tires,
> One the earnest looking forward,
>   One the hope our God inspires:
>
> One the gladness of rejoicing
>   On the far eternal shore,
> Where the One Almighty Father
>   Reigns in love for evermore.

Praise to the Holiest in the height
Lead, kindly light

'THE CARDINAL'S ECUMENICAL HYMNS
WHICH SO MANY LOVE'

If you were asked what is probably the best-known Roman Catholic hymn, included in pretty well every Protestant hymn book, what would you answer? Almost certainly you would have to say Cardinal Newman's *Praise to the Holiest in the height*, a fine hymn for any season.

Like another hymn found in many collections the world over, *Firmly I believe and truly*, the verses of *Praise to the Holiest* come from Newman's great poem *The Dream of Gerontius*, immortalized by Elgar's music – 'the best of me', the composer said himself. Strangely enough, Newman at first thought very little of *The Dream* and in fact is reputed at one time to have thrown it in the wastepaper basket! Fortunately it was rescued by a friend and published in a church magazine. The work tells the story of the soul's journey after death, and the actual verses of our hymn come as Gerontius enters into the presence of Emmanuel, where they are sung by the 'Fifth Choir of Angelicals'.

It was published in 1865 and only three years later, as the English hymnodist Dr Percy Dearmer, General Editor of *Songs of Praise Discussed*, said, the hymn was being sung by countless choirs of Evangelicals! John Bacchus Dykes' famous tune, which he called 'Gerontius', had not a little to do with this, as Newman freely admitted. Both hymn and tune became universally popular; *Praise to the Holiest* was a great favourite of Prime Minister Gladstone and sung at his funeral when he died in 1898.

Praise to the Holiest is a fine example of the way in

which a hymn can have a firm basis of fundamental Christian doctrine as its backbone and yet express it in majestic language so as to command widespread acceptance.

> O loving wisdom of our God!
> When all was sin and shame,
> A second Adam to the fight
> And to the rescue came.

Newman, of course, began his spiritual pilgrimage as an Anglican and was a dominant figure with Pusey and Keble in the Tractarian movement. Unlike his two contemporaries, however, Newman joined the Roman Catholic Church but was a man of such sincerity and stature that by the time of his death in 1890 most of the bitterness caused by his secession had been forgotten. Certainly his hymn is a splendid example of the way in which all Christians – Roman Catholic, Anglican, or Free Church – can find their true unity together at Calvary.

Lead, kindly light is Newman's other famous hymn. Indeed, not so long ago it would have ranked as the most popular hymn, Catholic or Protestant alike, and it was chosen as the ecumenical hymn *par excellence* for the 'Parliament of Religions' at Chicago in the 1880s. It was Queen Victoria's favourite and was read to her as she lay dying at Osborne. The story behind its composition is very romantic indeed. In 1833, some twelve years before he became a Roman Catholic, Newman, still a young man, was returning to England and suffered a serious illness in Sicily. It was before the days of steam and the boat in which he was sailing to Marseilles was becalmed for several days in the Straits of Bonifacio between the islands of Sardinia and Corsica. As darkness fell a single light pierced through the gloom from the harbour ahead and taking up his notepad Newman penned the words which became the hymn. He was in a crisis of doubt and uncertainty and the doubt expressed itself in the words he wrote:

> Lead, kindly light, amid the encircling gloom,
>   Lead thou me on;
> The night is dark, and I am far from home,
>   Lead thou me on.
> Keep thou my feet; I do not ask to see
> The distant scene; one step enough for me.

Many thousands of souls have responded to the same uncertainty in these lines: 'The distant scene' is well-nigh impossible for any of us to predict – 'one step enough for me'. ('Not for tomorrow and its needs – just for today!')

When Newman returned to Oxford he was in the congregation when John Keble preached his famous Assize sermon against national apostasy, in St Mary's in 1833 – the date agreed by everyone for the start of the great Tractarian revival which was to revolutionize the Church of England from top to bottom.

Many remember Newman's lovely prayer 'O Lord, support us all the day long of this troublous life . . .', and have found it a great comfort when experiencing the loss of those nearest and dearest to them. The last verse of his hymn says it all:

> So long thy power hath blest me, sure it still
>   Will lead me on,
> O'er moor and fen, o'er crag and torrent, till
>   The night is gone;
> And with the morn those angel faces smile,
> Which I have loved long since, and lost awhile.

John Bacchus Dykes composed the tune, 'Lux benigna', by which the hymn became famous, but as always there is no absolute rule as to the tune – many preferred, and still prefer, Charles Purday's 'Sandon', whilst others opt for

'Alberta', which was written by Sir William Harris when travelling in Canada in the 1920s. He was organist at St George's Chapel, Windsor, Director of the Royal College of Church Music, and edited the new hymnal for the Church in Wales, *Emynau'r Eglwys*, in 1952.

Praise to the Lord, the Almighty, the King of creation

'THE SONG OF PRAISE FROM LUTHER'S GERMANY'

We have many fine hymns from German sources, but one which has become increasingly popular in recent years is the seventeenth-century *Lobe den Herren*:

> Praise to the Lord, the Almighty, the King
> of creation;
> O my soul, praise him, for he is thy health
> and salvation;
>> All ye who hear,
>> Now to his temple draw near,
> Joining in glad adoration.

The author was Joachim Neander, who was born in Bremen in 1650. After a somewhat riotous student life he changed his ways and became a tutor, first at Frankfurt and then at Heidelberg, and was the Rector of the Latin School of Dusseldorf, during which time he wrote most of his hymns. A man of outstanding talents, he was not only a theological scholar but accomplished in both letters and music. Indeed he wrote some 60 hymns in all and composed their tunes. (One of his best-known tunes to English congregations is appropriately called 'Neander' and sung to the hymn *Come, ye faithful, raise the anthem*.) He was cut down by tuberculosis when he was only 30 and died in 1680.

Whilst at Frankfurt Neander met Philipp Jakob Spener, the founder of the 'Pietist' movement (a kind of early Methodism) in the Lutheran Church. The Pietists wanted to infuse new life into the lifeless official Protestantism of their time. There were house meetings, prayer and Bible study groups but, as with early Methodism, there was no attempt to break away from the parent Church. Peter Gerhardt, another notable hymnodist of the same period, was also a member of the group, and his and Neander's hymns helped to spread its ideals far and wide. Neander's own Pietism was combined with an intense love of the beauties of nature and it is this which comes out very vividly in the verses of *Praise to the Lord*. The hymn is based on Psalms 103 and 150, and the lovely English translation is by Catherine Winkworth. It first appeared in her *Chorale Book for England* in 1863 and Neander's tune was then somewhat adapted to its present form by the musical editors of that book, the distinguished Victorian composers Sterndale Bennett and Otto Goldschmidt.

You have no doubt sung them frequently before, but it is worth stopping for a moment to consider the intrinsic beauty of Neander's words, strong in his personal conviction and faith and yet a magnificent hymn of praise which can genuinely lift up the hearts of the countless thousands to have sung it since his untimely death.

> Praise to the Lord, O let all that is in me
>   adore him!
> All that hath life and breath come now with
>   praises before him!
>   Let the amen
>   Sound from his people again:
> Gladly for aye we adore him!

Silent night, holy night

'STILLE NACHT'

There must be few parts of the world that do not hear at Christmastide the familiar strains of a carol which was the result of collaboration between a poetic curate and a former weaver, neither of whom produced anything else which seems to have survived.

Franz Xaver Gruber was born in Unterweisburg in Upper Austria on 25 November 1787, and was apprenticed to the loom along with his family of weavers. The village organist, who was also the schoolmaster, became his tutor in the evenings for composition and organ-playing. By the time he was 28, Gruber had obtained a position as schoolmaster and organist at Oberndorf to the North of Salzburg and it was here his association began with the young curate Joseph Mohr. To quote Franz Gruber: 'Father Joseph Mohr gave me a poem which he requested I set to suitable music for two solo voices, chorus and a guitar accompaniment.' This became the carol *Stille Nacht – Silent night, holy night*.

That same evening – Christmas Eve 1818 – the new composition was sung for the first time in St Nicholas Church, the two men taking the solo parts to the accompaniment of the guitar. Little could they have known then that one day their carol would be sung in many different languages around the world. Apparently, at that Christmas of 1818, the organ was undergoing repair and the organ-builder was so impressed with the simplicity of *Stille Nacht* that he took a copy back to his village of Fügen in Zillertal, where his friends were instrumental in increasing its popularity.

Franz Gruber subsequently became organist and choir-master at Hallein and there founded the famous Hallein Choral Society, of which he was director from 1833 until his death in June 1863. His grave, placed outside his house, lies near to the church and is today a much-visited shrine. Joseph Mohr, who came from Salzburg and was five years younger, died fifteen years before Gruber, while he was assistant priest in Wagrein.

Sing, my tongue, the glorious battle
The royal banners forward go
Hail thee, Festival Day
(Welcome morning of joy)

'THE MOST FAMOUS HYMN-WRITER IN CHRISTENDOM'

Well – who would you say it is? I have no hesitation about my choice. It is the sixth-century Bishop Venantius Honorius Fortunatus. Born in Italy, a contemporary of Pope Gregory the Great, he was without doubt the best poet of his age, one of the great 'troubadours' – poet composers, mostly noblemen, who developed poetry based on contemporary Gregorian notation of plainsong, emanating largely from Southern France and Northern Italy. Bishop Fortunatus was well educated and a great friend of the saintly Queen Radegunde. Inspired by the stories of the discovery of the Saviour's cross by St Helena and living at the Abbey of the Cross at Poitiers, he gave to the Church two magnificent and inspiring hymns of the Passion. The first is *The royal banners forward go* and the other, *Sing, my tongue, the glorious battle*.

As always, the translations I prefer are those of John Mason Neale, and there are not really any tunes for them which work as well as the original plainsong, which somehow catches the spirit of the words so vividly that each year as Passiontide comes round, there is, for me at least, an inspiration that is both at once entirely objective and yet truly heartfelt, with a direct appeal to the emotions. Bishop Fortunatus wrote his great hymn *The royal banners* in AD 569 for the procession to the cathedral from the city gates of the Relic of the True Cross presented to Poitiers by Queen Radegunde, who had in turn been given it by the Empress Sophia of Constantinople. Is there anything to equal the lines of the fourth verse?

> O Tree of glory, Tree most fair,
> Ordained those holy limbs to bear,
> How bright in purple robe it stood,
> The purple of the Saviour's blood!

Or, in *Sing, my tongue*, consider verse 5:

> Faithful Cross! above all other,
> One and only noble tree!
> None in foliage, none in blossom,
> None in fruit thy peer may be;
> Sweetest wood and sweetest iron!
> Sweetest weight is hung on thee.

The ecumenical popularity of these hymns is conveyed by the Methodist writer Frederick Gill, who says in *The Glorious Company*: 'Fortunatus in his hymns has an almost unrivalled quality of power and devotion. The themes are lofty, the language is clear and closely knit, there is no weak sentiment or superficial emotion, and the effect is strong and stimulating. Always it was the Cross which symbolized his faith and evoked his finest poetry.'

But this remarkable writer, like all good Christians, did not end his religion with a full stop at Good Friday. For the joyful Easter morning, he bursts out into the jubilant greeting of *Hail thee, Festival Day* (or *Welcome, morning of joy!*) – and any church which does not consider using this on Easter morning is missing out badly. For this hymn, the plainsong is still available but it is our own Vaughan Williams who provided us with one of the best hymn tunes written in the twentieth century, 'Salve Festa Dies'.

> Lo, the fair beauty of earth, from the death of the
>   winter arising,
> Every good gift of the year now with its Master
>   returns.

Stand up, stand up for Jesus

'THE MIGHTY CONFLICT'

This is a hymn of Christian action which concerns an American Episcopal rector and his Presbyterian friend.

Back in the middle of last century the Revd Dudley Atkins Tyng was Rector of the Church of the Epiphany in Philadelphia and got into serious trouble with his congregation because of his bold denunciation of slavery, which he described as a major sin. It was at a time when not all Christians were so enlightened and many of his congregation themselves owned slaves, as was the common practice. Indeed they were so indignant at such politics from the pulpit that the Rector was forced to relinquish his parish and carry on his ministry in a hall in the city, where his forceful preaching attracted great crowds, culminating in one vast gathering attended by over 5,000, 1,000 of whom subsequently signed a pledge of conversion. On the Wednesday after this memorable Sunday, Mr Tyng met with a most tragic accident on a nearby farm: his arm was caught in some machinery and literally wrenched off, and he died within a few days. As he was dying, his friend the Revd George Duffield, a Presbyterian minister, asked him if he would like to send a last message to his congregation and Tyng replied: 'Yes, tell them to stand up for Jesus'.

George Duffield was much moved and when he was asked to preach at the funeral service he not only chose his text from Ephesians – 'Stand therefore, having your loins girded about with truth' – but at the end of his address he read some verses he had composed, based on his friend's memorable last message:

Stand up, stand up for Jesus,
Ye soldiers of the Cross!

> Lift high his royal banner,
>> It must not suffer loss.
> From victory unto victory
>> His army he shall lead,
> Till every foe is vanquished,
>> And Christ is Lord indeed.

'Morning light', the tune to which this popular hymn is most often sung, also has something of a history, in that it started life as a secular song, ''Tis dawn, the lark is singing'. It was composed by George James Webb in 1837. Its martial rhythm seems to fit Duffield's verses admirably and so *Stand up, stand up for Jesus* has become a universal favourite.

Another appealing feature of the story is that George Duffield seems to have spent his entire ministry building up small congregations and churches which needed his help. He could afford to do this as he was a man of some considerable private means. He also edited the Christian family newspaper *Christian Observer*, which enjoyed quite a following at that time.

Today the words of the hymn which he inspired have lost nothing of their significance, and probably as never before there is now the need for all Christian believers to stand up and be counted if we are to be true soldiers of the cross.

Take my life and let it be

'THE HOLIDAY VISIT THAT PRODUCED A FINE HYMN'

Miss Frances Ridley Havergal, daughter of the Rector of Astley, Worcestershire, was born in 1836 and died in 1879. A gifted poet and musician, she has bequeathed to us several fine hymns, with pride of place generally given to one she wrote during a holiday visit to friends when she was 37. She wrote in her diary that, unable to sleep, she mused on the theme of consecration and found herself putting together some twelve couplets involving the whole of her life – words, deeds, will, intellect, the whole self. Subsequently her father joined the couplets into six four-line stanzas and wrote a tune for them which, appropriately, he called 'Consecration'. Frances began: 'Take my life and let it be, consecrated Lord to thee'. The following verses ranged widely, asking God to take hands, feet, lips, intellect, heart, will, personal belongings, and, finally, in the last verse, 'Take my love', to culminate in the line that sums it all up, 'Ever, only, all for thee'.

Writing subsequently to a friend, Miss Havergal described the method by which her hymns 'came to her': 'For me, writing is praying and I feel just like a child who asks "What am I to do next?" ' She went on to say that it was the Holy Spirit who answered her query and inspired the words she wrote.

Frances certainly demonstrated her dedication to her work, becoming fluent in Latin, Greek, Hebrew, French, German and Italian – the latter she mastered largely while on afternoon walks! Quite a remarkable woman one way and another and we are all indebted to her more than a century later as we still sing her purposeful words, that God will indeed take our lives, like hers, and consecrate them to his service.

111

Tell me the old, old story

'THE GOSPEL STORY'

> Tell me the old, old story
>   of unseen things above,
> Of Jesus and his glory,
>   of Jesus and his love.
> Tell me the story simply
> As to a little child,
> For I am weak, and weary,
> And helpless, and defiled.

This hymn, which is especially loved by older gener-
ations, was written by Arabella Catherine Hankey
(born 1834 and died 1911) a member of the so-called
Clapham Sect. Like the Wesleys, she came from a very
large family but was a very reserved person and led what
many would consider today to be a very quiet life, until
she went to South Africa to bring home her brother
who had been wounded there during the Boer War.
The long journey at that time was a great adventure,
especially for someone so little experienced in travel,
and involved going a great distance up-country after the
sea voyage from England. She was much impressed by
the witness and work of the clergy and missionaries
whom she met and this led her in turn to devote the
rest of her life to what were then called 'foreign mis-
sions'. When she returned to London she became
involved in the work of the church in the parish where
she was living. Her vicar, the Revd G. H. Wilkinson
(later Bishop of Truro), became a much-valued pastor
and friend.

Few people today who sing her hymn would know that
it was originally written only as an introduction to a series
of verses published in 1868 telling the whole story of the

gospel from the time of the Garden of Eden to our Lord's resurrection and Pentecost, and repeating the challenge to each individual to bear witness to Christ. It certainly appealed at the time to a great many and had a large circulation. Translated into several languages, it was much used in the mission field in both Africa and Asia.

Catherine wrote many other hymns which have not stood the test of time, but *Tell me the old, old story* has endured, partly because of the popularity of its tune, which was written by Dr W. H. Doane, an American composer of several popular hymn tunges. He attended a convention of the YMCA at Montreal in Canada where he heard Major General Russell introduce Catherine Hankey's newly published verses and they affected him profoundly.

Afterwards, he had to visit the White Mountains in New Hampshire, USA, and wrote the tune which has become so memorable whilst he was making his long journey by stage-coach. Dr Doane altered the hymn somewhat by using verses of eight lines each, introducing a refrain after each verse. Catherine did not like this at all, maintaining that the verses were adequate on their own, but the new setting became so popular that in the end she consented to let it stand.

When I was Summer Chaplain at the English Church on Lake Como (1980–1992), we often sang this hymn at our ecumenical 'Songs of Praise' on Sunday evening:

> Tell me the story softly,
> With earnest tones and grave;
> Remember, I'm the sinner
> Whom Jesus came to save.
> Tell me that story always,
> If you would really be
> In any time of trouble
> A comforter to me:

Tell me the old, old story
Of Jesus and his love.

Tell me the same old story
When you have cause to fear
That this world's empty glory
Is costing me too dear.
Yes, and when that world's glory
Shall dawn upon my soul,
Tell me the old, old story,
'Christ Jesus makes thee whole'
Tell me the old, old story
Of Jesus and his love.

Tell out, my soul, the greatness of the Lord

'A MODERN MAGNIFICAT'

One of the real casualties of the liturgical movement which has established the Holy Communion Service as the principal act of Sunday worship in many churches up and down the land is the loss of the services of Morning and Evening Prayer with their essentially scriptural background of Psalms, Canticles and Lessons. It is said that 'Good Pope John' was asked in the 1960s what he admired most in the Anglican tradition and he replied promptly: 'Prayer Book Evensong'. It is at Matins and Evensong that we rehearse the gospel Canticles of the Benedictus, Magnificat and Nunc Dimittis. Today there are all too many who have never even heard of them, which is why the hymn by Timothy Dudley-Smith (Bishop of Thetford until 1992), *Tell out, my soul, the greatness of the Lord*, is specially welcome. It is an essentially modern version of the Magnificat, inspired by the New English Bible, and the hymn has already become well established although it was only written in 1961. John Betjeman saw it as 'one of the few new hymns of recent years that could be commended', and most of us will agree with Sir John.

Tell out, my soul, the greatness of the Lord:
   Unnumbered blessings give my spirit voice;
Tender to me the promise of his word;
   In God my Saviour shall my heart rejoice.

Tell out my soul the greatness of his name:
   Make known his might, the deeds his arm has done;
His mercy sure, from age to age the same;
   His holy name, the Lord, the Mighty One.

Tell out, my soul, the greatness of his might!
   Powers and dominions lay their glory by;

Proud hearts and stubborn wills are put to flight,
  The hungry fed, the humble lifted high.

One good reason why the hymn has become so popular is one of the fine tunes to which is is sung – 'Woodlands', composed by W. Greatorex, who was the music master at Gresham's School (he died in 1949). It is absolutely wedded to the Bishop's words and, as Cyril Taylor, Editor of the *BBC Hymn Book*, says in *Hymns for Today Discussed* (1984), is within everyone's grasp – irresistible.

The Church's one foundation

'THE WINDSOR CURATE'S FIRM FOUNDATION'

Dr Winnington Ingram, Bishop of London for close on 40 years in the first part of our century, used to say that he had lived on a diet of cold chicken and one particular hymn for as long as he could remember. He meant that his frequent Confirmation services took him to many vicarages for supper where cold chicken was almost invariably on the menu and that, almost without exception, the last hymn would be *The Church's one foundation*.

I suppose you can have too much of a good thing, even with episcopal suppers and hymns, but the good Bishop's experience did pay tribute to the remarkable popularity of a fine hymn which first appeared in 1836, then some seven verses long. The author was Samuel John Stone (1839–1900), at the time a curate at Windsor, a zealous and enthusiastic churchman who went on to become a well-known figure of his day as Rector of All Hallows-on-the-Wall, in the City, and a noted hymnographer, a member of the first committee of *Hymns Ancient and Modern*. His most famous hymn was written as a contribution to quite a famous theological controversy of the period. In South Africa, Bishop Colenso of Natal was thought to have preached heresy by questioning some of the basic biblical and traditional doctrines of the Church. Ranged against Bishop Colenso was his brother South African, Bishop Gray of Capetown, and our Windsor curate, much admiring and applauding the latter's defence of orthodoxy, wrote *The Church's one foundation* as a tribute to him. The obvious reference to the dispute comes in verse 3 of the original:

The Church shall never perish;
    Her dear Lord, to defend,
To guide, sustain and cherish
    Is with her to the end:
Though there be those who hate her
    And false sons in her pale
Against or foe or traitor
    She ever shall prevail.

The first part of verse 4 (verse 3 in today's hymnals) obviously goes on to refer to the dispute also:

Though with a scornful wonder
    Men see her sore oppressed,
By schisms rent asunder,
    By heresies distressed.

The Church's one foundation was used as the processional hymn in Westminster Abbey at the opening service of the first Lambeth Conference in 1867. It is a remarkably fine hymn, whatever its original motive, and has been taken by the whole Church everywhere as part and parcel of our regular worship. It has the genius of expressing basic Christian teaching in a concise yet simple and dignified way:

Elect from every nation,
    Yet one o'er all the earth,
Her charter of salvation,
    One Lord, one Faith, one Birth,

and:

Yet she on earth hath union
    With God the Three in One,
And mystic sweet communion
    With those whose rest is won:
O happy ones and holy!
    Lord give us grace that we,

118

> Like them, the meek and lowly,
>   On high may dwell with Thee.

So far as I know, there has only ever been one generally accepted tune for Stone's words. It is called 'Aurelia' and was composed by the great Samuel Sebastian Wesley, originally, it seems, for *Jerusalem the golden*. The most inspiring rendering I have experienced was in Detroit, Michigan, when I attended the Convention of the Episcopal Church in the USA. They sang it as a processional hymn whilst all the delegates literally marched in at a really rollicking pace, at about twice the speed I have ever heard it sung in England!

The day thou gavest, Lord, is ended

'CHOSEN FOR THE GREAT QUEEN'S JUBILEE'

So what is your favourite evening hymn? There are so many lovely evening hymns to choose from, all of them firm favourites. It is very strange therefore that one which commands widespread affection was not really intended by its author for eventide at all. It is John Ellerton's *The day thou gavest, Lord, is ended*. He was quite a prolific Victorian hymn-writer and collaborated with Bishop Walsham How (author of *For all the saints*) in publishing SPCK's *Church Hymns* in 1881. Ellerton's hymns composed or translated specifically for evening use included *O strength and stay upholding all creation* and *Saviour, again to thy dear name we raise*. Born in London, he served his first curacy in Eastbourne, following his ordination in 1850. Afterwards he became Rector of Barnes and died (at 66) in Torquay in 1893 on 15 June.

Ellerton had been honoured by having one of his hymns chosen by Queen Victoria herself to be sung at her Diamond Jubilee service in St Paul's Cathedral, not for its evening theme at all but because she regarded it as the ideal 'Empire' hymn. It was, of course, *The day thou gavest* with its world-wide missionary message so appropriate for the occasion when so much of the world's map was coloured red and the sun never set on the British Empire!

> As o'er each continent and island
>   The dawn leads on another day,
> The voice of prayer is never silent,
>   Nor dies the strain of praise away.
>
> The sun which bids us rest is waking
>   Our brethren 'neath the western sky,
> And hour by hour fresh lips are making
>   Thy wondrous doings heard on high.

The tune 'St Clement' was specially written for Ellerton's lovely words by another clergyman, Clement Schole-field, who also started his ministry in Sussex, at Hove Parish Church.

As far as John Ellerton's churchmanship went, he claimed he was a 'Liberal, High-Church Evangelical' – quite something in Victorian times, let alone today! And he is to be admired for his strong belief that there should be no copyright where hymns, either words or music, were concerned, saying they belonged to the whole Church. Even in the heyday of 'Empire' he got both his politics and his theology right too – we all know how *The day thou gavest* ends:

> So be it, Lord! thy throne shall never,
>   Like earth's proud empires, pass away;
> The kingdom stands, and grows for ever,
>   Till all thy creatures own thy sway.

The duteous day now closeth

'THE FIELDS OF EVERLASTING LIFE'

One of the very finest hymns I know of in the beautiful English rendering set to music harmonized by Johann Sebastian Bach is from Germany: *Nun ruhen alle Walder, The duteous day now closeth*. I say 'rendering' deliberately, for when he included it in his famous *Yattendon Hymnal* in 1899, Robert Bridges, later (in 1913) to be made Poet Laureate, paraphrased rather than translated the German of the author Paulus Gerhardt (1607–1676), the Lutheran Archdeacon of Lübben. Bridges produced a truly magnificent English poem in its own right:

> Now all the heavenly splendour
> Breaks forth in starlight tender
>   From myriad worlds unknown;
> And man, the marvel seeing,
> Forgets his selfish being,
>   For joy of beauty not his own.
>
> Awhile his mortal blindness
> May miss God's loving-kindness,
>   And grope in faithless strife:
> But when life's day is over
> Shall death's fair night discover
>   The fields of everlasting life.

The tune 'Innsbruck' (the harmony is from Bach's *St Matthew Passion*) was originally a secular folk song, noted by Heinrich Isaac in 1598.

Verse 4 of *The duteous day now closeth* is probably best of all – the closing lines are inscribed on my family's grave in Udimore churchyard:

> His care he drowneth yonder,
> Lost in the abyss of wonder;

To heaven his soul doth steal:
This life he disesteemeth,
The day it is that dreameth,
That doth from truth his vision steal.

The head that once was crowned with thorns

'THE ASCENSIONTIDE HYMN FROM DUBLIN'

There will be few churches where, as Ascensiontide comes round each year, they will not sing the ever popular hymn for this season: *The head that once was crowned with thorns*. It admirably sums up the joy and triumph of the King of Glory, replacing the crown of the Passion with the 'royal diadem'.

> The highest place that heaven affords
>   Is his, is his by right,
> The King of kings and Lord of lords,
>   And heaven's eternal light.

The lovely words first appeared in 1820, just five years after the Battle of Waterloo. The author was Thomas Kelly, son of an Irish judge. Ordained in the Anglican Church in 1792, he was subsequently barred by Dr Fowler, then Archbishop of Dublin, because of his extreme evangelical views, and became an Independent minister. Poverty was rife and, having private means, Kelly did all he could to help. To quote Norman Mable:

> 'As an illustration of the high regard the 'down-and-outs' had for their benefactor, a good story is told of a particularly necessitious couple who were in dire circumstances. The husband endeavoured to cheer up his forlorn wife by exclaiming, 'Hould up Bridget, bedad. Sure and Mr Kelly will pull us out of the bog even if we are sinking in for the last time.'

Kelly was the author of 756 hymns in all, though only three have withstood the test of time. First there is the fine Passiontide hymn *We sing the praise of him who died*. Then comes the Easter hymn *The Lord is risen indeed, now*

is his work performed and finally the Ascensiontide choice.
The latter is invariably sung to a tune called 'St Magnus',
which was composed by the great Jeremiah Clarke of
'Trumpet Voluntary' fame, organist of St Paul's Cathedral at the end of the seventeenth century. Words and
music are well matched and convey the sense of joy and
triumph as the Church salutes her glorified Lord. Whatever the differences in human affairs, we may now rejoice
that both the Archbishop of Dublin and Thomas Kelly –
and Jeremiah Clarke – join with angels and archangels
and all the company of heaven in adoration of 'Him who
died upon the cross' and rose again and is alive for
evermore.

The King of Love my Shepherd is
The Lord's my Shepherd, I'll not want
The God of love my Shepherd is

'EVERYONE'S FAVOURITE'

He died on 12 February 1877, a clergyman baronet who was a great hymn-writer and who will always be remembered so long as Christians sing his lovely verses – some his own originals, others superb translations from the ancient Latin and Greek. He was Henry Williams Baker, eldest son of Admiral of the Fleet Sir Henry Loraine Baker. Born in 1821, Baker succeeded to the baronetcy in 1859. He had been ordained in the Anglican ministry some fifteen years previously and become Vicar of Monkland, Herefordshire, in 1851, where he remained for 26 years. Hymnody was his great love and he became the first chairman of the group who published the earliest edition of *Hymns Ancient and Modern* in 1859. Baker also included a number of other hymns, such as *Lord, thy word abideth* and *Shall we not love thee, Mother dear*, which was thought to be very High Church at the time and caused him to be accused of 'popery'.

Baker's greatest triumph was his really beautiful paraphrase of the most popular of psalms, Psalm 23. Is there anybody who does not know and love *The King of love my Shepherd is*? It remains almost universally popular, despite other fine renderings, such as the Scottish metrical version, *The Lord's my Shepherd, I'll not want* (sung to the popular air, 'Crimond', at the wedding of Queen Elizabeth (then Princess) and the Duke of Edinburgh). There is also George Herbert's *The God of love my Shepherd is*, written two centuries earlier than Baker's hymn, but very similar to it in several ways, for both make a deliberate 'Christianization' of the Old Testament original – the 'still waters' of the Psalmist become 'streams of living water', and there is a specific link with Holy Communion in the fifth verse: 'Thy pure chalice'.

The tune most commonly used and loved for *The King of love* is 'Dominus regit me', the title taken from the Latin for the opening of Psalm 23. It was composed by the famous John Bacchus Dykes, who was responsible for no less than 100 tunes in *Hymns Ancient and Modern*, including some of the most popular and well known. He was Precentor of Durham Cathedral and a very High Churchman for his time. His taste for coloured stoles and the 'eastward position' for celebrating Communion brought him into conflict with his Bishop!

The tune 'Crimond' is usually attributed to Jessie Irvine, whose father was Minister of the Kirk at Crimond (in Aberdeenshire) for 30 years or more. The joyful tune 'University' is used for George Herbert's *The God of love, my Shepherd is*. It comes from John Randall's *Psalms and Hymns* (1794).

As Henry Williams Baker lay dying, when only 56, he was heard reciting the third verse of his famous hymn:

> Perverse and foolish oft I strayed;
>   But yet in love he sought me,
> And on his shoulder gently laid,
>   And home, rejoicing, brought me.

Indeed, we can all join with him in making his last verse into a heartfelt prayer:

> And so through all the length of days
>   Thy goodness faileth never:
> Good Shepherd, may I sing thy praise
>   Within thy house for ever.

Thine be the glory, risen, conquering Son

'THE CONQUERING HERO'

When it comes to assessing the popularity of any hymn, more often than not it is the tune which proves to be the determining factor just as much as the words themselves. Certainly this is the case when we take such a fine tune as the triumphal march 'See the Conquering Hero Comes', from Handel's oratorio *Judas Maccabaeus*, composed in 1746. Set to the words of *Thine be the glory, risen, conquering Son*, it clothes one of our finest modern Easter hymns in a majestic manner, admirably suited to the Eastertide theme. It speaks to us afresh of the joy of the new life which springtime brings to the natural world around us, and also of that 'Glorious hope of everlasting life' which is the heart of the gospel message.

The words of *Thine be the glory* were first written in French by Edmond Budry, the pastor of the Protestant Church at Vevey in Switzerland: *A toi La Gloire O Ressuscité*. It was included in *Lausanne Hymns*, published in 1904, but it was only when Richard Hoyle, then Baptist minister at Kingston-on-Thames, translated Budry's French into English that *Thine be the glory* became justly popular in the best sense of the word. Now it is sung everywhere by Catholic and Protestant alike.

It is a truly stalwart affirmation of our Christian faith and hope and we may indeed be thankful to the three men who gave us this great Eastertide hymn: Edmond Budry (1854–1932), Richard Hoyle (1875–1939), and George Frederick Handel (1685–1759), himself a devout believer and the composer not only of *Judas Maccabaeus* and much besides, but also of the *Messiah*, one of the greatest Christian choral works of all time.

Through all the changing scenes of life
As pants the hart for cooling streams
While shepherds watched their flocks by night

'METRICAL PSALMS AND GOSPEL PARAPHRASE'

The original hymns of the Jewish people were the Psalms of David, inherited in due course by the Christian Church and used in worship down the ages. Then in the sixteenth century the first metrical version of the Psalms appeared in Geneva (1562) and in England the first complete metrical version was also published in 1562. One of these, Psalm 100, became the familiar Old Hundredth (*All people that on earth do dwell*), whose tune was written by Louis Bourgeois with words by William Kethe. The 'Old Version', as it was called, lasted for over 130 years until the 'New Version' of the Psalms – *Fitted to the tunes used in Churches* – was published in 1696. It was the work of two Irish clergymen: Nicholas Brady and Nahum Tate. Brady became Chaplain both to William and Mary and to Queen Anne. Tate was made Poet Laureate in 1692. He was a strange character; the poet Alexander Pope referred to him as 'Poor Tate – always a sorrowful appearance and in a terrible muddle', and Robert Southey as 'the lowest of the Laureates'. He was always poor and died penniless, embarrassingly and unexpectedly whilst hiding from his creditors in the Royal Mint in 1715. He wrote many poems – one of them entitled 'Panacea – a Poem on Tea' – and also 'edited' Shakespeare so that even the tragedies such as *King Lear* and *Hamlet* were given happy endings!

But Tate also gave us three really fine hymns which are justly as popular today as when they were first written: *Through all the changing scenes of life, As pants the hart for cooling streams*, and the familiar Christmas carol, *While shepherds watched their flocks by night*. The first two are metrical settings of Psalms 34 and 42, and another is a paraphrase of the gospel story from Luke (2.8–17). There were at first no less than ten verses for *Through all the changing scenes of life*. After verse 3 came:

> Their drooping hearts were soon refreshed
> > Who looked to him for aid,
> Desired success in every face,
> > A cheerful air displayed.

The first half of the hymn ended:

> While hungry lions lack their prey,
> > The Lord will food provide,
> For such as put their trust in him
> And see their needs supply'd.

Surely Pope and Southey's criticisms of Tate were a little unfair, as the words of 'As pants the hart' are really quite impressive:

> Why restless, why cast down, my soul?
> > Hope still, and thou shalt sing
> The praise of him who is thy God,
> > Thy health's eternal spring.

The tune for *Through all the changing scenes of life* is 'Wiltshire', composed by Sir George Thomas Smart in 1795. He was organist of the Chapel Royal and wrote music for the coronations of both William IV and Queen Victoria. He also conducted the first performance of Mendelssohn's oratorio, *St Paul*, at Liverpool in 1836. The tune sung usually for *While shepherds watched their flocks* is known as 'Winchester Old' and first appeared in the Psalter of Thomas Este (*The Whole Book of Psalms*) in 1592.

Thy hand, O God, has guided

'OUR CHRISTIAN HERITAGE'

One of the great hymns speaking of the Christian tradition of Great Britain was written by Dr Edward Plumptre for the 1889 supplement of *Hymns Ancient and Modern*. He was a Dean of Wells Cathedral and a contemporary of the great Dean Church of St Paul's, who was a distinguished scholar of his day and Fellow of Oriel College, Oxford, where he was closely associated with Newman, Pusey and Keble and the leaders of the Oxford Tractarian movement. Dean Plumptre based his verses on Ephesians 4.4–6, where the Apostle speaks of 'One Lord, one faith, one baptism, one God and Father of all'. He was sufficiently down to earth and realistic to take a responsible view of church history and to recognize the facts both good and bad in its chequered existence from the earliest times to the present day. The hymn he wrote begins:

Thy hand, O God, has guided
Thy flock from age to age,
The wondrous tale is written,
Full clear, on every page.

The author looks back to the first period of English history – when 'Thy heralds brought glad tidings/To greatest as to least' – recalling the epic tales of Columba of Iona, and Aidan of Lindisfarne and those who first established the Church in our land. But he also describes the bad times – 'Through many a day of darkness/Through many a scene of strife' – bearing in mind the Commonwealth period and Cromwell's military dictatorship when the Prayer Book was banned, the churches used as stables for army horses, and the king himself beheaded. Then the hymn comes round full circle: 'And we, shall we be faithless?/Shall hearts fail, hands hang down?' Dean Plumptre was thinking of the challenge to the faith in his own day towards the end of the nineteenth century. What would he have thought of the Church now, in our own time, beset with so many and perhaps even greater problems? He would, I am sure, have had just the same message for us:

> And we, shall we be faithless?
> Shall hearts fail, hands hang down?
> Shall we evade the conflict,
> And cast away our crown?
> Not so; in God's deep counsels
> Some better thing is stored;
> We will maintain, unflinching,
> One Church, one Faith, one Lord.

We must never forget that it is God's Church, not ours, that Christ said at Caesarea Philippi, 'I, [not you] will build my Church and the gates of hell shall never prevail against it':

> Thy mercy will not fail us,
> Nor leave thy work undone;
> With thy right hand to help us,
> The victory shall be won;
> And then, by men and angels
> Thy name shall be adored,
> And this shall be their anthem,
> 'One Church, one Faith, one Lord'.

The tune nearly always set for Dean Plumptre's hymn is 'Thornbury', an inspiring melody composed by a great Church musician, Basil Harwood, organist both of Ely and Oxford Cathedrals, who wrote it for the London Church Choirs Festival in 1898. 'Thornbury' is often sung also these days to *O Jesus, I have promised* (see pages 91–2). Harwood also gave us the tune 'Luckington', which we all love to sing to George Herbert's *Let all the world in every corner sing*.

We can all heed the words of the Epistle for Saints Simon and Jude's Day (28 October), where we are bidden to contend earnestly for the faith once delivered to the Saints.

'GOOD NEWS FOR ALL'

One distinctly twentieth-century hymn which has already become firmly established in the regular use of many church congregations is *We have a gospel to proclaim*. Its author is Canon Edward Joseph Burns, born in 1938. He wrote the six verses to support an evangelistic campaign in his diocese of Blackburn when each deanery was called to a Renewal of Faith by the Bishop in 1968. The hymn was originally suggested to him by the tune 'Fulda', the very fine and catchy melody to which it is usually sung. It was composed by William Gardiner and published in his *Sacred Melodies* in 1815. He was a very talented musician, son of a wealthy Lancashire stocking manufacturer.

Canon Burns sets out the fundamentals of the Christian gospel in four verses:

> Tell of his birth at Bethlehem
>   Not in a royal house or hall
> But in a stable dark and dim,
>   The Word made flesh, a light for all.
>
> Tell of his death at Calvary,
>   Hated by those he came to save,
> In lonely suffering on the Cross;
>   For all he loved his life he gave.
>
> Tell of that glorious Easter morn:
>   Empty the tomb, for he was free.
> He broke the power of death and hell
>   That we might share his victory.
>
> Tell of his reign at God's right hand,
>   By all creation glorified.

He sends his Spirit on his Church
    To live for him, the Lamb who died.

It is not difficult to predict that, like several other hymns in this book classified as 'moderns', Canon Burns' *We have a gospel to proclaim* will last and be sung for many a long year to come.

Now we rejoice to name him King:
    Jesus is Lord of all the earth.
This gospel-message we proclaim:
    We sing his glory, tell his worth.

We plough the fields, and scatter

'ALL GOOD GIFTS AROUND US'

Every autumn our churches echo to the sound of Harvest hymns and amongst them are the ever-popular verses we know from earliest childhood: *We plough the fields, and scatter*. How many of us will know, however, that they are of German origin?

This hymn has a most fascinating history, beginning in a village festival in Northern Germany (1782) when it was written for a sketch called 'Paul Erdmann's Fest' by Matthias Claudius (born in 1740, he died in the year of Waterloo: 1815). Claudius included a peasant song of some seventeen four-lined stanzas which he heard on a local farm, and in 1800 these became the hymn largely as we know it today. Claudius was a son of a Lutheran pastor and was, at the time he wrote the original verses, Commissioner of Agriculture and Editor of the local paper at Hesse Darmstadt. He was also a great friend of the poet Goethe. Whilst at university he became an atheist for a time but later regained his Christian faith.

The English translation is by Jane Montgomery Campbell (1817–1878), herself a vicar's daughter and translator of many German hymns. She was a music teacher who died tragically in an accident while driving on Dartmoor.

The familiar tune 'Wir Pflugen' was composed by Johann Schulz (1747–1800) who was Kappel-Meister (choirmaster) first to Prince Henry of Prussia in Dresden and afterwards at the Court of Denmark in Copenhagen. He travelled widely through Germany, France and Italy.

According to Dr Ian Bradley, in the *Penguin Book of Hymns*, the hymn as we know it has now been updated as follows:

We plough the fields with tractors,
    With drills we sow the land:
But growth is still the wondrous gift
    Of God's almighty hand;
We add our fertilizers
    To help the growing grain,
But for its full fruition
    It needs God's sun and rain.

Sir John Betjeman in turn parodied it: 'We spray the fields, and scatter the poison on the ground'.

Most of us, however, hold fast to the original version and ask that God will accept our gifts with 'that which thou desirest/Our humble, thankful hearts'.

When all thy mercies, O my God

'MR ADDISON'

A hymn which is a particular favourite of mine comes from the time of Queen Anne, whose reign, you will recall, is described in the old song 'The Vicar of Bray' as 'the Church of England's glory'.

In 1672 a new baby arrived at Milstons Rectory in Wiltshire and the Rector, the Revd Lancelot Addison (afterwards Dean of Lichfield) and his wife decided to christen their son Joseph. He was destined to become famous for his association with *The Spectator* and *The Tatler*, and to make his mark as one of the greatest of English essayists. Some of his essays concluded with what he called 'pieces of divine poetry' and one particular essay is called 'Gratitude'. He wrote: 'Every blessing we enjoy, by what means soever it may be derived, is the gift of Him who is the great Author of all good, the Father of all mercies'. The verses which followed began:

> When all thy mercies, O my God,
>   My rising soul surveys,
> Transported with the view, I'm lost,
>   In wonder, love, and praise.
>
> Unnumbered comforts to my soul
>   Thy tender care bestowed,
> Before my infant heart conceived
>   From whom those comforts flowed.

These words have found their way into nearly all Christian hymnals, majestic in language yet amply expressing the simple trust and thankfulness of every believer, no matter how unlettered or highly educated. The same could be said for Addison's other great hymns, *The spacious firmament on high* and *The Lord my pasture shall prepare.* Certainly his verses seem to sum up our human experience just as adequately for us all in Queen Elizabeth II's reign as for those in that of Queen Anne.

Addison died in 1719, just five years after his Queen. John Wesley said of him: 'God raised up Mr Addison to show the excellence of Christianity and Christian institutions'. If, when our time comes, such can be said of us, even if we are not able to write beautiful hymns, we can surely ask for no finer memorial. Let Mr Addison have the last word for all of us:

> Through every period of my life
> Thy goodness I'll pursue,
> And after death in distant worlds
> The glorious theme renew.
>
> Through all eternity to thee
> A joyful song I'll raise,
> For O! eternity's too short
> To utter all thy praise.

Ouseley's fine tune 'Contemplation' is just right for *All thy mercies* and much preferable to other tunes sometimes set.

When I survey the wondrous cross

'A PASSIONTIDE HYMN'

One Sunday morning the Watts family returned from their Southampton church. Isaac, the oldest of the nine Watts children, complained about the poor quality of the hymns that were sung. 'Then give us something better, young man', his father replied.

Isaac rose to the challenge and wrote a hymn beginning 'Behold the glories of the Lamb'. So a comparative youngster of only nineteen went on for some half a century writing many wonderful hymns which historically have earned him the title 'Father of English Hymnody'. *How bright these glorious spirits shine, O God, our help in ages past, Come, let us join our cheerful songs, Jesus shall reign where'er the sun* are all Watts hymns. His most famous hymn, which has become part and parcel of our Christian heritage, is *When I survey the wondrous cross*, based on Galatians 6.14. It can justly be described as the affirmation of the very central truth of our faith. There are probably few churches where this magnificent hymn is not sung each Passiontide.

Many of us know the words by heart from our youth up, as did the great Dr Thomas Arnold of Rugby School. He sang it himself one Good Friday (1842) and afterwards was overheard repeating to himself the words of the third verse: 'See from his head, his hands, his feet/Sorrow and love flow mingled down'. He probably did not know at the time that before that particular Good Friday ended he would be called into the presence of that same crucified and risen Lord.

Watts remained a 'Dissenter' all his life, yet now his bust stands in Westminster Abbey and no one can possibly dissent from his wonderful concept of the cross of Christ expressing that 'Love so amazing, so divine' that it 'demands my soul, my life, my all'. So we remember Isaac Watts not only for his great faith but because, rather than being simply content to criticize what he thought was poor and unworthy, he set out to put something better in its place. (See also pages 61–2.)

'Rockingham' is the tune invariably sung in Britain for this famous hymn, and was adapted by Edward Miller, organist at Doncaster Parish Church (1756–1807), from Webbe's *Collection of Psalm-Tunes* (1820). You may hear another tune in Wales. If you have been fortunate enough to hear the tune 'Morte Criste' sung by the Welsh choirs in the Albert Hall on St David's Day you will know that it is a very fine and moving tune.

'THE SHROPSHIRE LAD WHO TURNED DOWN A BISHOPRIC'

'Read any of them; they are all good' advised Dr Johnson. He was referring to the writings of the great seventeenth-century Puritan divine Richard Baxter, and Dr Johnson's advice is usually worth taking.

Born in Shropshire in the year before Shakespeare died (1615), Baxter was destined to become one of the foremost religious figures of his age and a man who moreover turned down the chance to become Bishop of Hereford rather than compromise his conscience. He always claimed to have been converted by a tract bought at the door from a passing pedlar. He was ordained and appointed 'Lecturer' at Kidderminster Parish Church, which he found almost empty. No less than five extra galleries were added during his time there to accommodate the great crowds that came to hear him preach.

During the Civil war he served as chaplain in Cromwell's army but this did not deter him from rebuking General Oliver later on when he assumed supreme power and became a military dictator. Baxter strongly questioned episcopacy as then constituted and took part in the unsuccessful Savoy conference of 1661 to amend the Prayer Book so that the Presbyterians could remain members of the Established Church, but they were not accepted, and so when the Act of Uniformity came in 1662, Baxter was one of the 2,000 or more clergy turned out from their livings. In fact he was successfully brought before the notorious Judge Jeffreys and imprisoned, but released two years later. He died in 1691 at the age of 76.

Baxter was an enthusiastic ecumenist long before his time. He formed the Worcestershire Association of Ministers and through it made a gallant attempt to carry out a scheme of unity between Anglicans, Presbyterians and Independents. But it is his poetry and hymnody that we are most concerned with here, of course, and amongst these is one of the most popular hymns in the English language: *Ye holy angels bright*. Originally there were some sixteen stanzas and the hymn was included in the *Poor Man's Family Book* which Baxter published in 1672, with a 'Request to Landlords and . . . Rich Men to give to their Tenants and Poor Neighbours'. The hymn was called a *Psalm of Praise* and had verse headings of 'Angels', 'The gloried saints', 'The World', 'The Church' and 'My Soul'. These were edited and to some extent rewritten by John Hampden Gurney for his *Collection of Hymns* (1838), which is why in many hymnals the authorship is given as 'Richard Baxter and Others'. It is still sung today to the inspiring melody of 'Darwall's 148th' and deservedly remains a favourite for all denominations, which would surely have pleased the ecumenical Richard.

> My soul, bear thou thy part,
>   Triumph in God above,
> And with a well-tuned heart
>   Sing thou the songs of love.
>   Let all thy days
>   Till life shall end,
>   Whate'er he send,
>   Be filled with praise.

BIBLIOGRAPHY

Some sources consulted and recommended for further reading.

Bradley, I. (ed.) *Penguin Book of Hymns*. Penguin Books, 1990.

The Church of Ireland Gazette. Lisburn, Co. Antrim, 25 February 1994.

Colquhoun, F., *Sing to the Lord*. Hodder and Stoughton, 1988.

Colquhoun, F. (ed.), *Your Favourite Songs of Praise*. Oxford University Press/BBC, 1987.

Colquhoun, F., *More Preaching on Favourite Hymns*. Mowbray, 1990.

Cross, F. L. (ed.), *Oxford Dictionary of the Christian Church*. Oxford University Press, 1958.

English Hymnal. Oxford University Press, 1906.

Frost, M. (ed.), *Historical Companion to Hymns Ancient and Modern*. Proprietors of *Hymns Ancient and Modern*, 1962.

Gill, F. C., *The Glorious Company*. Epworth Press, 1958.

The Hymnal Companion 1940. Church Pension Fund, New York, 1956.

Hymns Old and New (with supplement). Kevin Mayhew, 1991.

Hymns Ancient and Modern Revised. William Clowes and Sons, 1950.

Hymns and Psalms. Methodist Publishing House, 1983.

Jefferson, H. A. L., *Hymns in Christian Worship*. Rockliffe, 1950.

Limmer-Sheppard, W. J., *Great Hymns and Their Stories*. Epworth Press, 1950.

Lovell, E. W., *A Green Hill Far Away*. Friends of St Columb's Cathedral, Derry, 1994.

Mable, N., *Popular Hymns and Their Writers*. Independent Press, 1944.

Mission Praise. Marshall, Morgan and Scott, 1983.

New Standard Hymns Ancient and Modern. Proprietors of *Hymns Ancient and Modern*, 1983.

New English Hymnal. Canterbury Press, 1986.

Oxford Book of Carols. Oxford University Press, 1969.

Songs of Praise. Oxford University Press, 1931.

Taylor, C., *Hymns for Today Discussed*. Canterbury Press and Royal School of Church Music, 1984.

Whittle, T., *Solid Joys and Lasting Treasure*. Ross Anderson Publications, 1985.

INDEX OF HYMNS AND TUNES

(Names of tunes in bold)

INDEX OF AUTHORS AND TRANSLATORS, COMPOSERS AND ARRANGERS

(Composers and arrangers in italics)